HOW (NOT) TO TALK
ABOUT EUROPE

Sunder Katwala
and Steve Ballinger

BRITISH FUTURE

PUBLISHED BY
British Future
Kean house
6 Kean Street
London WC2B 4AS

AUTHORS
Sunder Katwala and Steve Ballinger

EDITOR
Steve Ballinger

Design by Soapbox Design

Printed by Smith and Watts Ltd

© British Future 2016
ISBN 978-0-9931202-1-3

The moral rights of the authors have been asserted.

ABOUT BRITISH FUTURE:
British Future is an independent, non-partisan thinktank engaging people's hopes and fears about integration and migration, opportunity and identity, so that we share a confident and welcoming Britain, inclusive and fair to all.

www.britishfuture.org
Tel. +44 (0) 20 7632 9069
Twitter: @BritishFuture

CONTENTS

ACKNOWLEDGEMENTS

The European Union referendum will give us all a say on one of the biggest questions facing Britain.

This pamphlet does not take a view about how people should cast their vote in the referendum. British Future is an independent and non-partisan think-tank and a registered charity: in *How (not) to talk about Europe* we seek to illuminate some of the key choices that will matter to those who have yet to make up their minds, and set out the challenges for those seeking to secure public consent for Britain to Remain in or Leave the EU.

This short pamphlet is not a comprehensive study of all aspects of the European Union or of Britain's place within it. There are many important issues – including the relationship between Eurozone and non-Euro members; climate change; foreign policy and Britain's place in the world – which are not covered here in any detail. Each of these could prove a crucial policy debate and each is likely to affect important outcomes, but they currently seem rather less likely to feature prominently as the decisive issues in the referendum choices of large sections of undecided voters, compared to the economic, immigration and identity challenges that we do discuss in more detail.

Throughout the pamphlet we refer to the two rival campaigns as 'In' and 'Out', 'Leave' and 'Remain'. These refer to the broad pro-EU and anti-EU movements that have continued to debate the issue of Britain's membership of the EU since the referendum of 1975 – and not specifically to the various 'Remain' and 'Leave' campaigns that were launched in the last 12 months.

The authors would like to thank British Future staff interns past and present, Joe Cryer and Naisha Hussain, for their work on this report; trustees Simon Clark and Alasdair Murray for their helpful comments on the text; and colleagues Elizabeth Gibson, Matthew Rhodes and Avaes Mohammad for their support.

Thanks to Deborah Mattinson and her colleagues at Britain Thinks, who conducted deliberative research for British Future on the EU and migration in Southampton in both November 2013 and March 2015, and to Universities UK for facilitating deliberative research on the EU in Sheffield and in East London in August 2015.

Our one-day workshop in Southampton, bringing together British-born and Polish-born local residents, was supported by the European Commission. Full editorial control remained with British Future and Britain Thinks.

We are grateful to the organisations who have either co-hosted events with us or invited us to speak on these themes to a range of different audiences, including: APPG on European Reform, APPG on Migration, Barrow Cadbury Trust, Bristol Festival of Ideas, Christians on the Left, ConservativeHome, Counterpoint, Demos, European Council on Foreign Relations, European Movement, Fabian Society, IPPR, Liberal Democrat European Group, London Chambers of Commerce, UK NARIC, National Institute of Economic and Social Research, Open Europe, Policy Network, PriceWaterhouseCoopers, Progress, ResPublica, Runnymede Trust, Southern Policy Centre, TUC and Universities UK.

We have learnt a lot from those engaged with this issue across both sides of the EU referendum debate: we would particularly thank Polly Billington, Stephen Booth, Margaret Burton, Douglas Carswell, Rosa Crawford, Rowenna Davis, Rob Ford, Paul Goodman, Matthew Goodwin, Phoebe Griffiths, Daniel Hannan, Susan Hitch, Mark Leonard, Julia Onslow-Cole, Marcus Roberts, Will Straw and Owen Tudor. Naturally, none of them is in any way responsible for any of the conclusions that the authors reach.

We would also like to thank ICM and Survation for their work polling public attitudes to the EU – details of the specific polls conducted for British Future can be found in Chapter 8. The report also draws on other attitudinal research in the public domain.

This pamphlet also draws on broader research on identity and immigration issues conducted for our 2014 publication *How to Talk About Immigration*.

Sunder Katwala and Steve Ballinger
December 2015

EXECUTIVE SUMMARY

The referendum on Britain's membership of the European Union will loom large over the politics of 2016.

It is a referendum that is up for grabs, for either side. Our research finds the public split almost down the middle between 'In' and 'Out' and, perhaps more importantly, it finds that most voters have not yet made their minds up. Many don't know which way they will vote and of those that do, most are 'leaning' one way or another but still yet to make a final decision. This is particularly true of certain sections of the voting public, such as women and younger voters, whose final decision – both on whether to vote at all and which choice to make if they do – may decide the referendum outcome.

Both 'In' and 'Out' campaigns have a strong core support – but neither amounts to more than 20% of the public. Voters who are currently undecided about the referendum will therefore decide its result. Both campaigns will need to try to persuade them onside in order to win – and yet neither is succeeding in doing so. The arguments and messages from prominent voices for both 'In' and 'Out' may resonate with existing supporters but their arguments do not cut through to the undecided voters whom they need to persuade. In fact, the messages deployed by both sides can actively repel the very voters that they need to attract.

The same is true of the messengers voicing these arguments. Our research finds that two of the most prominent voices in the EU debate – Nigel Farage for 'Out' and Tony Blair for 'In' – are the two politicians least-trusted by the public on the EU debate.

We propose in this report that voices for both 'In' and 'Out' need to change their tune if they want a hearing from the voters who will decide the referendum. *How (not) to talk about Europe* suggests ways in which they might do so.

For 'In' this means more than just playing on people's fears about Brexit. It will require pro-EU advocates to make a positive case for Britain in Europe that resonates with voters emotionally – one that embraces our history and the symbols of British identity – rather than the fact-based case upon which they tend to rely.

A further challenge for 'In' is to engage with voters' concerns about immigration from the European Union under free movement rules – a topic they would prefer to leave well alone. But both sides need to set out a real-world vision of what immigration would look like if they win the referendum. Pro-EU voices need to concede that immigration is unlikely to be substantially reduced while we have free movement, and set out a plan to manage relatively high levels of migration better – such as by using the tax receipts from an expanded workforce to ease the pressures brought by migration to places where change has been rapid.

The 'Out' campaign, too, has challenges of its own on immigration. While this issue is the primary concern for some of its core support, voters who aren't already onside may be turned off if the case for 'Out' appears to be about immigration and nothing else. Do that, and the campaign could encounter the same 'Purple ceiling' that UKIP hit in the General Election. But 'Out' has another immigration challenge too – in telling voters what a post-Brexit Britain would look like, it will need to answer some important questions: could Britain still enjoy free trade with Europe without free movement? What becomes of EU citizens already here? And what about immigration from outside the EU?

A more pressing concern for the 'Out' campaign, however, is to tackle the uncertainty that people feel about a change to the status quo. Eurosceptics will need to show that they have a viable plan for what Britain would look like post-Brexit. And they too face challenges in engaging with voters' strongly-felt sense of identity: 'Out' will need to demonstrate that it is comfortable with modern Britain, and does not want to turn back the clock, if it is to appeal to younger voters, to ethnic minorities and to women.

The impact of our referendum choice on the economy is another key factor for voters, who want an answer to the question *'Which will leave me better off, in or out?'* While both sides will have to contest this, we suggest that neither is likely to land a knockout blow with one killer fact, due to the sheer volume of conflicting factual information with which voters will be bombarded during the referendum campaign. This is a particular challenge for 'In', who will be looking to win the economic argument. For 'Out', neutralising its impact on voting may be all they need to do.

The two opposing campaigns are not the only voices in this referendum, however. Business should, we suggest, overcome its instincts to duck the debate and should instead engage productively – before they are forced into doing so by their duties to inform shareholders, staff and customers. Business can play a useful role in the debate if it speaks to the public interest from its particular locus of expertise, posing questions to the 'In' and 'Out' campaigns, informing the debate and informing voters' personal choice rather than telling them which way to vote.

The referendum is a big moment for Britain and, if conducted well, it could also have a positive impact on our politics. Whichever side wins, the referendum is likely to have a profound effect on discussion of immigration in the UK. It could mark the end of a debate that is primarily about numbers – because the public will have been given an opportunity to put at least a chance of significantly reducing numbers on the agenda.

It could also, as did the independence referendum in Scotland, breathe new life into public democratic engagement. And while this referendum will provoke disagreement it will also highlight the common ground on which we all agree.

A referendum that's good for Britain means one in which as many people as possible have their say. It should also be one in which voters have a clear idea of what they are voting for. To this end we propose a 'Third Campaign' to broaden engagement and increase participation in the referendum. That could mean that Britain comes to a conclusive decision, as a nation, on an issue that has dogged our politics for a quarter-century.

INTRODUCTION – HOW (NOT) TO TALK ABOUT EUROPE

The EU Referendum looks likely to be the biggest moment of this Parliament, perhaps of several Parliaments.

It is an important moment for the country, a chance for all British voters to have their say on a question that has raged for a generation. It is right that it should be decided this way, by popular vote: much of the public is fed up with a politics in which they are told that they do not have a choice. On issues like globalisation, immigration and austerity there has been little option for voters to have their say – leading to UKIP's populist 'revolt on the right' and perhaps a second 'revolt on the left' in the rise of Jeremy Corbyn to the Labour leadership. The referendum will offer voters a choice between two clear and competing options for their country.

For such a big decision, however, there is at present a remarkably low degree of public engagement. Most people don't yet know for sure which way they will vote in the referendum, and we should expect the polls to veer quite drastically one way and another over the coming months. Many people won't decide until a week or two before the vote; many more remain unconvinced that the EU has much bearing on their everyday life and may not vote at all.

For a highly-engaged minority, that statement could not be further from the truth. They have been having this argument for 25 years, some for 40 years since the last referendum. Back in 2014, when British Future asked the public to state what the most important event of the year was for them, UKIP voters put the European elections above the football World Cup. (Though in the end, the party's electoral performance was markedly better than that of England's footballers).

> *For a quarter-century these two competing sides have been fighting a battle among themselves and yet have failed to convince, in many cases even to engage, the wider public.*

It is quite remarkable that for a quarter-century these two competing sides have been fighting a battle among themselves and yet have failed to convince, in many cases even to engage, the wider public. That is particularly true of women and younger voters: one might expect both campaigns to be actively courting such 'up for grabs' voters who are markedly less decided than, for example, older men; and yet the most prominent voices for both 'In' and 'Out' campaigns remain predominantly older and male.

Now both sides in the referendum have no choice but to find a way to appeal to the wider, EU-indifferent public, if they are to exceed the 50% share of the vote that will push them over the finishing line.

Winning standing ovations from one's own supporters can be distracting, intoxicating even. The problem is that from the stage, you fail to notice that only the front row is clapping. Further back, people are shuffling in their seats and checking their phones. Twice as many people think 'In' campaigners are out of touch with ordinary people than think they understand their concerns; twice as many think 'Out' has a negative agenda than a positive one.

So a change of tune is required. Both sides need to learn how NOT to talk about Europe – to reach beyond their comfort zone and engage unconvinced voters with their arguments, whether they are for or against Britain's membership of the EU.

The early moves from the campaigns on both sides suggest many of those involved understand that they will need to reach out and to persuade a majority. The campaign will be more of a marathon than a sprint; many of the undecided voters may well, sensibly, choose to engage much closer to the moment of decision. Both the 'Remain' and 'Leave' campaigns will face a tricky task as they seek to mobilise their support and begin to build the broader campaigns they need. The evidence of this report suggests that the winning campaign could well be whichever side does the most to disrupt expectations, surprising people with its ability to broaden its appeal. That means both campaigns may need to surprise their supporters too – or at least take them on a journey about how to win the argument with those not already onside. Otherwise, if and when they get their pitch to the public right, the campaigners might risk a chorus of complaint from their most active supporters, those who would find a narrower pitch more compelling.

This challenge for both 'Leave' and 'Remain' with their current base of support is increased because a referendum campaign is not like a General Election. The official 'Remain' and 'Leave' campaigns will only be part of the eco-system of a broader national argument about the EU. There will be much less command-and-control message discipline of MPs and party candidates than there is in a party campaign, where political careers often depend on not upsetting their party leaders. Both sides will need to be part of a broader network of support, including those with different political and economic views, but will want their allies to help build support rather than to inadvertently lose it.

These campaigns cannot control their supporters; so they will instead have to influence them about how to make the case in the way that helps the cause to win. The logic suggests that the two campaigns should be unusually transparent about what they are saying and doing and why. Instead of the old political model of keeping the secrets of the campaign war-room to themselves, so as to mount guerrilla attacks on the opposition, a successful 'network campaign' on either side needs to do a great deal to engage, especially early on this year ahead of the final 'short campaign', in an open conversation with their own supporters about how the case needs to be pursued, if it is to secure the majority consent of the British people for the goal that they share.

There are some who would rather they didn't have to go through with this process at all. Some Europhiles, notably including former Prime Minister Tony Blair, think that Britain's membership of the EU is far too important to trust to the public – that it is too big a risk to give voters a say on the question because they might vote 'Out'. Others on the Eurosceptic side also appear worried that they might lose and find that their favourite argument is no longer one that anyone else wants to have. Debates over wording, timing and who gets to vote may be preparing the ground for a rejection of the result as unfair and a demand for another go.

> "Modern Britain may have its flaws but most people think it's a pretty good place to live – and both campaigns will need to remember this."

Fearing the referendum is pointless. It is happening whether one likes it or not. And while some may be sincere in their practical or constitutional opposition to it, doing so smacks somewhat of a lack of confidence in their own arguments, too: if the case is strong enough, they should be able to convince others of its worth. Moreover, it is contemptuous of democracy. People have a right to participate in a decision of such significance to the country and campaigners from both sides should grasp this opportunity to win the argument, once and for all.

Doing so may bring additional and unexpected benefits. Offering people a clear choice, on a big issue, with a tangible outcome could revitalise our democracy – much as the 2014 referendum did in Scotland. It will also, in settling a question on which there is disagreement, tell us much about the things upon which we can all agree.

In seeking the support of more than half the electorate, both campaigns will be obliged to occupy the common ground on which most of us concur: that we have a proud, positive and inclusive national identity; that Britain is part of the global economy, open to the wider world; and that our basic value of 'fair play' means we'll give a fair chance to those who come here to contribute and become part of our society.

Modern Britain may have its flaws but most people think it's a pretty good place to live – and both campaigns will need to remember this. Those who'd like to take us back to the 1950s will find that most people don't want to come with them: we are now wealthier, healthier, smarter, more equal and more connected with the world. But others who are embarrassed or dismissive of the things that make us uniquely British, rather than European, will get an equally cold shoulder from the public. Our history, language, culture and manners – and the symbols we use to celebrate them – are held dear at a deeply emotional level.

So a question about Europe will also tell us a lot about Britain. Both sides will need to present their answer to the whole of Britain if they want to come out on top.

It's going to be a big deal, and a big choice – and it looks like it might be close.

PART I

THE REFERENDUM CHALLENGE

1. *UP FOR GRABS*: A FUTURE HISTORY OF HOW THE REFERENDUM WAS WON AND LOST

More than half the public hasn't made its mind up yet about the EU referendum.

Polling by ICM for British Future shows both 'In' and 'Out' pretty much neck-and-neck in the referendum race. 44% of people say they are either certain to vote 'out' (19%) or 'leaning out' (25%) while 42% are either certain to vote 'in' (17%) or 'leaning in' (25%).

With 14% of saying they don't know, that leaves around two-thirds (64%) of the vote up for grabs, either wholly undecided or leaning one way or the other but waiting for more information before they decide which way to vote.

These are voters who will decide whether Britain leaves the EU or stays in the club – and that decision could go either way.

Figure 1: Thinking about a possible referendum on Britain's EU membership, which of the following best sums up your current voting intention?

% of respondents in, out and leaning

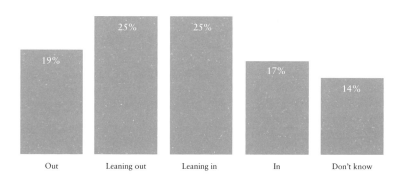

There are a host of factors that could tip their decision in either direction. The balance is as it should be – open for both sides to make a convincing case for Britain. So this is a referendum that remains very much up for grabs, for both 'In' and 'Out'.

A LOOK INTO THE CRYSTAL BALL – FOUR ALTERNATIVE REFERENDUM FUTURES

What the papers could say

I – PURPLE RAIN

"I never meant to cause you any sorrow... I never meant to cause you any pain..." As Prince's 1984 hit rang out over every news bulletin, Britain voted yesterday to leave the European Union on the wettest Thursday in a decade.

The torrential downpour meant only those who really cared about Europe, one way or the other, bothered to vote. Turnout for the referendum on Britain's membership of the European Union was just 49% – 22 million people. Some disgruntled 'in' voters have already started to question the legitimacy of the result. Some have even publicly blamed TV schedulers for keeping people at home – though as UKIP's Nigel Farage was quick to retort, 'Out' voters seemed to be capable of recording the 'Bake Off'.

With the margin of victory so narrow, 51% to 49%, every vote counted. Farage's call to 'Break out your brollies, break out of the EU' mobilised the core Eurosceptic vote who had backed UKIP in numbers in 2014's European elections.

Boris Johnson's surprise decision to lead the Conservative 'Out' campaign presented a more liberal, metropolitan vision of a post-Brexit Britain: open for business with India and China, breaking free of the sclerotic economies of the EU but fused with a flag-waving patriotism that the 'In' campaign struggled to understand, let alone replicate.

Campaigners for Britain to remain part of the EU simply failed to give undecided voters leaning 'in' – particularly middle-class women and younger people – a reason to care enough to brave the weather. With the Labour Party still seemingly more interested in fighting itself than its political opponents, Labour supporters received mixed messages about whether the party was 'in' or 'out'.

The 'Lexit' proposal of Owen Jones and the TUC, borrowing the language of Greece's Syriza to oppose EU corporatism and erosion of workers' rights, succeeded in mobilising the Labour Left and some students to vote to leave the EU. Russell Brand's pro-Europe 'EUtube' broadcasts from a squat in Amsterdam may have persuaded some of his million+ online followers to turn up and vote the other way, but not enough to swing the result. Brand was unavailable for comment on the result yesterday.

Voters in Scotland – where extreme weather warnings prompted accusations that the Met Office was meddling in politics – bucked the trend and voted 'In' by 56% to 44%. While their numbers weren't enough to change the overall result, SNP leader Nicola Sturgeon has already hinted that a second referendum on Scotland's membership of the United Kingdom could be an inevitable consequence of Britain's decision to leave Europe. Many of her MPs are suggesting that they should press for an early ballot in the hope that Scotland can in some way inherit Britain's EU membership.

Pressure is now growing on Prime Minister David Cameron to step down and make way for a new leader to keep post-EU Britain together. Boris Johnson has kept his counsel so far, but it is surely only a matter of time before the former Mayor of London throws his hat in the ring. With George Osborne and Theresa May both backing the losing side this time, bookmakers have installed Boris as the favourite to succeed Cameron as Conservative Party leader and PM. Johnson was reportedly seen dining with Tory Party donors last night.

II – BRITAIN'S GOT EURO FEVER

It may be an exaggeration to say that two footballers kept Britain in the EU.

But Wayne Rooney's decisive penalty in England's Euro 2016 semi-final victory over Germany this summer, and a Gareth Bale hat-trick that secured Wales an historic place in the last eight, may have played a part.

Scenes of 'Euro Fever' followed as thousands ignored security concerns and hopped over the channel to watch the two British teams, with pictures of fans partying together in the streets providing just the European mood music that the 'In' campaign wanted. Bale even praised the EU free movement rules that smoothed his move to Spain's Real Madrid.

Prime Minister David Cameron will claim that his own interventions were somewhat more decisive in securing victory in the referendum, by a margin of 65% to 35%. Together with Chancellor George Osborne, hotly tipped to succeed Cameron when he steps down in the next year, the PM led a disciplined campaign to stay in the EU, at the head of a Conservative Party that remained remarkably united.

It helped that many MPs, expecting Cameron to come back almost entirely empty-handed from Brussels, were pleasantly surprised by the few concessions that the Prime Minister managed to extract from Brussels. A Twitter-based campaign by human rights lawyers and liberal celebrities, opposing the proposed restriction of child benefit to UK-resident children, also helped to rally the Tory troops behind their man.

As a result, only 30 anti-EU Conservative MPs backed the 'Out' campaign, leaving Nigel

Farage to take centre stage as by far the most prominent Eurosceptic voice.

Much has been made of Farage's role in this referendum. Dogged by comparisons with defeated US Republican leadership candidate Donald Trump, Farage dominated this debate, sparking complaints that he was given too much airtime. And while Eurosceptics may appreciate his work ethic, the post-mortem is unlikely to look favourably on the UKIP leader.

His on-air meltdown at Andrea Dumescu, a Romanian migrant whose quietly-spoken question caused a visibly-exhausted Farage to lose his temper live on *Question Time*, was seen by some as a pivotal moment in the campaign. It helped that Dumescu was a children's nurse, not to mention particularly photogenic: when her tears were broadcast across the country, people sided with the pretty NHS worker over the red-faced politician.

Labour leader Jeremy Corbyn kept a low profile during this referendum campaign, speaking little of his personal Euroscepticism. This may have preserved his fragile leadership for now. But prominent campaigning for 'In' by Labour's frontbench refuseniks Tristram Hunt, Chuka Umunna and Yvette Cooper have been seen by Labour insiders as the beginnings of a scramble for the leadership post-Corbyn.

Most agree that the referendum has been good news for Britain's democracy. Turnout, at 65%, was higher than most expected. And young people, who showed little interest in the General Election of 2015, became more engaged with politics. Universities and Youtube campaigners have been credited with convincing them to vote and have their say in a decision that will affect their future.

That looks likely to have provided a significant boost for 'In'. Likewise in Scotland, where three-quarters of eligible voters cast a ballot, most of them in favour of Britain remaining in the EU. The UK-wide result will, however, have quashed Nationalist hopes for a second referendum on Scotland's place in the Union.

Nigel Farage and Nicola Sturgeon may not be happy, but David Cameron and George Osborne certainly are. The people of Britain have provided a decisive answer to the question that has dogged their party for decades.

III – AN UNCERTAIN AND TEMPORARY TRUCE

This was a knife-edge referendum. The 'In' campaign scraped a narrow victory last night in a vote marred by controversy and negative campaigning. With only two percentage points separating the two sides, commentators and pollsters are seeking explanations. Defeated campaigners are seeking scapegoats.

Theories abound as to what tipped the balance. Many commentators highlight the gender gap, with men splitting 50-50 but women voting 'in' by 57% to 43%. Fingers have been pointed at the 'blokeish' presentation and lack of prominent women in the Eurosceptic campaign. This has sparked some calls within UKIP to raise the profile of Deputy Chair Suzanne Evans. Other Eurosceptic commentators have blamed the defeat on the 'Out' campaign's keen focus on immigration. Some voters – young people and ethnic minorities in particular – didn't like the message or the tone of the 'Out' campaign and voted the other way. They weren't persuaded by the efforts of Eurosceptics Douglas Carswell MP and Dan Hannan MEP to present a more positive vision of a stronger Britain thriving outside the EU.

Some Eurosceptics are crying foul and have vowed to keep up their fight. A *Daily Express* online poll this morning, showing a slim win for 'Out' when voters were asked a differently-worded referendum question, has prompted angry Eurosceptic campaigners to vent their frustration on social media under the #EUStitchUp banner. There have even been calls for the result to be declared void.

'In' campaigners, however, are breathing a sigh of relief. The role of opinion polls is under scrutiny once again, having convinced many Europhiles that they were miles (or Kilometres) ahead. When the exit poll declared the race too close to call, there was visible panic among 'In' campaigners, who feared a "Shy 'Brexit" effect. Some are saying that Prime Minister David Cameron repeated the mistakes of Scotland all over again: complacent for most of the campaign, panicky at the end. In response, No10 has been keen to emphasise Cameron's record: two referendums, with a General Election majority in between for good measure, makes him the PM who kept Britain together *and* in Europe.

While some Tory backbenchers are saying he should now step down swiftly and leave on a high, a growing body of Conservative MPs is starting to question the wisdom of letting a proven winner go before the 2020 election.

That's not what potential successors George Osborne, Theresa May, Sajid Javid and Boris Johnson want to hear. All have praised the PM for his win, though Boris in particular has been at pains to emphasise his own prominent role in securing the referendum result.

IV – THE SWING OUT SISTERS

Britain decided to leave the European Union last night, by a clear margin. The "Out" campaign secured 17.5 million votes while just 11.5 million voted for Britain to remain in the EU. Senior Conservatives last night questioned how long David Cameron can now remain as Prime Minister after losing a referendum of his own making.

It was the last of many surprises in a campaign that began with a clear lead in the polls for the 'In' campaign. The economic meltdown in the Eurozone, precipitated by Greece's default, probably tipped the balance. The pro-EU campaign's focus on fears for the post-Brexit economy backfired as Europe suddenly looked like an equally risky bet.

The personalities of this referendum also played a major part. Theresa May's decision to defy Cameron and lead the 'Out' campaign may be the political masterstroke that took Britain out of the EU and takes her into Number 10 Downing Street. With the *Daily Mail* and *Telegraph* both dubbing 'Maggie May' as the party's next Margaret Thatcher, she is now odds-on to take the top job.

Together with UKIP leader Suzanne Evans, who took over the leadership of the Eurosceptic party after Farage's surprise decision to take a back seat, the two 'Swing Out Sisters', as they became known, prompted a sharp spike in 'Out' support among women voters, who had previously shunned the 'blokeish' campaign to leave the EU.

Ousted Labour Leader Jeremy Corbyn, still smarting from the coup by Labour MPs that installed Tom Watson in his place, also played a part in yesterday's historic decision. When Corbyn spoke out against the EU and aligned his left-wing 'Momentum' movement with the 'Lexit' project of Owen Jones and trade unions, he ensured that 'Out' became a campaign that spanned the political divide from right to left.

The 'Remain' campaign never matched their combined appeal. Its main weapon, Prime Minister David Cameron, was hamstrung by his failure to secure any concrete concessions from a poorly-managed renegotiation. Former PM Tony Blair polled negatively with the public from Day One, yet remained prominent, together with Peter Mandelson, Michael Heseltine and representatives of the CBI, in a campaign that was criticized for being too elite and London-focused.

Richard Branson's admission that he 'still wouldn't rule out joining the Euro' undermined his credibility and that of the wider 'In' campaign. Suggestions that Europhiles would see Britain adopting the increasingly shaky EU currency dogged the 'In' campaign right to the end.

Across the country there was just one place that unequivocally backed the EU yesterday: London. As the capital struggles to comprehend the extent to which it has lost touch with the rest of the country, a host of columnists both left and right have threatened to leave the UK. #RepublicOfLondon has been trending on Twitter in the capital.

Exit polls suggest that Scotland – seen as strongly pro-EU before the vote – split 50/50, with significant Scottish support for the union-led 'progressive out' campaign. Nicola Sturgeon has so far remained silent on the question of a second independence referendum.

With half of Scotland seemingly in agreement with England, preserving the Union may be one less headache for Cameron. Preserving his legacy may be weighing rather more heavily on his mind right now.

2. *UNHAPPY FAMILIES*: WHO WILL DECIDE THE REFERENDUM?

In a referendum that could be close-run, and in which most voters have yet to make up their minds, the successful campaign will be the one that reaches beyond its core vote to the undecided voters and those who are 'leaning' in or out but are yet to fully decide which way to vote.

Just what deal the Prime Minister comes back with from Brussels, and how that is presented to voters, will make a significant difference to these 'leaners' who are waiting on David Cameron's negotiation before they make up their minds. More important still are the approaches taken by the two competing campaigns.

Whether the 'In' or 'Out' campaign succeeds in persuading the 'undecideds' will be key to determining the choice that Britain makes. Neither is making much headway so far: both pro-EU and anti-EU voices do well at reaching their core supporters who are already onside, but neither can feel comfortable that they will reach beyond 50% of the vote. Instead the 'In' camp swings from panic to complacency while 'Out' veers between over-confidence and defeatism.

Understanding the voters who will decide the election, and what motivates them, will be key to securing their support. For 'Out', the key issue is sovereignty, that "decisions affecting Britain should be made in Britain", closely followed by immigration. For 'In', the economy is by far the main issue influencing their decision, followed by ease of travel. That remains true whether voters are certain of their choice or 'leaning' one way or the other.

Figure 2: Why do people want to stay in or get out of the EU?

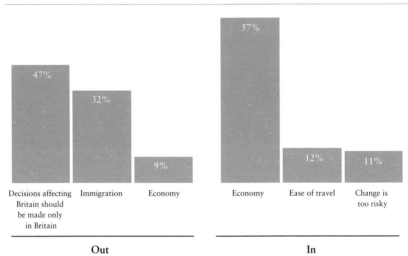

47%	32%	9%		57%	12%	11%
Decisions affecting Britain should be made only in Britain	Immigration	Economy		Economy	Ease of travel	Change is too risky
Out				**In**		

There are some clear trends: younger voters trend towards 'In' while older voters are more likely to vote 'Out'; people who finished education after secondary school are more likely to be Eurosceptic, while those with a university education are more likely to want Britain to remain in the EU.

When our researchers spoke to groups of East London students about the EU, it was striking how candid they were about not having given much thought to the referendum, even while recognising the importance of the choice that Britain makes. There was a clear sense among the group that they would need more information before they felt able to make a the choice; but equally that they did not know where that information might come from. Our 2015 *Voice of a Generation* project, which toured the country taking the views of first-time voters on the issues that mattered most to them, heard very little from young people about Britain's membership of the European Union.

This presents a challenge for both 'In' and 'Out' campaigns, in engaging younger voters sufficiently that they will use their votes.

But it is equally an opportunity: with younger people considerably more likely to be uncertain which they will vote in the referendum, this represents a significant number of 'up for grabs' votes for the campaign that succeeds in reaching this audience.

WOMEN WILL DECIDE THIS REFERENDUM – SO WHY ARE THE CAMPAIGNS ABOUT EUROPE SO BLOKEISH?

Women voters have the power to decide the EU referendum – if they choose to take it. That partly reflects a simple demographic fact: there are one million more women than men in Britain, mainly due to the gender gap in life expectancy.

But the bigger reason why both referendum campaigns need to persuade women voters is that women are considerably more likely to be undecided about Europe. Research shows that on the issue of Britain's EU membership, women are more open to changing their minds than men and also less certain whether or not to take part.

In most polls on the referendum question, just over 10 to 15% of men say they don't know how they will vote. For women that figure nearly doubles: 20–25% of them aren't sure.

Figure 3 The 'don't know' referendum gender gap

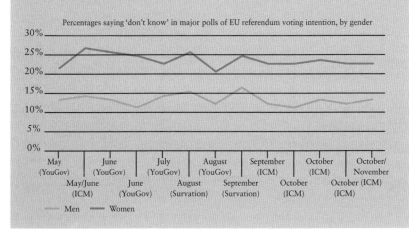

To put this in context, women are more likely than men to admit to uncertainty when polled on most issues. And there are also important differences, as one would expect, between different women – based on education, social class, geography and marital and employment status. But overall, the evidence still points to a potentially significant difference between men and women when it comes to their views of the EU and the referendum:

- Women are almost twice as likely to answer 'Don't Know' in most EU referendum polls.

- Women are less likely to say they are certain to vote in the referendum: 43% of men are certain which way they will vote, whether that's 'In' or 'Out'; that drops to just 29% of women.

- Women are considerably less persuaded by UKIP, and have been less likely to vote for them. When asked how much they trust a series of different politicians when they talk about Britain's membership of the EU, 41% of men say they trust Nigel Farage, but only 31% of women agree.

- Intriguingly, evidence suggests that women may be more Eurosceptic than men, and more difficult to persuade to vote for Leave.

Deborah Mattinson is an expert on public attitudes and founder of Britain Thinks, which has been speaking to women about Europe over the last 12 months. She writes:

When I listen to women talking about the Europe debate, what strikes me is their frustration at the way the different arguments are shaping up. They know this is an important decision, and want more information so they can make that choice when the referendum comes. But nobody really seems to be talking about what matters to them.

We know that women are undecided about the EU Referendum. They're less likely than men to express certainty on a whole range of issues. Crucially though, they're no less likely to vote – in fact there are more women voters than men. So there are millions of women's votes potentially up for grabs in the referendum. It's remarkable that the two campaigns aren't making more effort to go after them.

Voters will have heard very few female voices in the referendum campaign so far. One would hope that changes once the competing campaigns step up their outreach to the public. At the moment it all sounds removed from reality. The pro-European case looks like men in suits reeling off GDP figures and economic studies in a very abstract way that's quite alien to how most people think about the economy; the Eurosceptics can sound obsessed, as if anybody who didn't read every clause of every Treaty since Maastricht has no right to hold an opinion.

None of that is really going to strike a chord with women voters. In fact none of it is going to strike much of a chord with ordinary members of the public in general. Public voices on both sides of the EU debate are going to have to make their arguments much more 'human-friendly' if they want to win the support of undecided voters. We know, for example, that the 'stay' arguments are much more effective when related to the personal level – talking about potential job losses rather than impacts on trade and investment. For women these arguments are even more effective when framed in terms of job security for current and future generations, playing in to existing concerns about their children and grandchildren's prospects. Similarly, on opposing side, we see that the immigration argument packs the most punch when it relates to the impact of immigration on public services in voters' own localities, including ever growing pressure on schools and hospitals.

Each side is going to have to work much harder to make the 'human' case, but it's even more true for women voters – who may well decide the outcome of the referendum.

The evidence suggests both sides of the big Europe argument have struggled to find the voice that makes sense to most women.

The EU institutions remain dominated by middle-aged men in suits. The presidents of the Commission, the Eurogroup, the Central Bank and the European Parliament are all men. Indeed, every President of the European Commission to date has been male. The elected Parliament, which might be expected to do a bit better, last elected a woman president over a decade ago in 2002.

Britain's public debate about the European Union has been a very blokeish affair too. The 1975 campaigns reflected the male-dominated politics of the day, with only one or two women playing a prominent role. Forty years on, the country will surely expect the campaigns to be different. A glance at the most prominent voices in the opposing 'In' and 'Out' camps, however, is likely to leave them disappointed, with only Laura Sandys of the pro-EU European Movement and Kate Hoey of the Eurosceptic Labour for Britain standing out in a sea of male (and white) faces.

Both, however, will need to do more than increase female representation among their spokespeople if they want to reach women voters. The rival campaigns should be developing approaches that specifically appeal to particular groups of women whose votes may be 'up for grabs' to them.

The 'Leave' campaign has a challenge of persuading those women who are critical of the European Union to believe it is worth taking the risk to leave.

Across Europe, academic studies using Eurobarometer evidence[1] show that women are, if anything, mildly more sceptical towards European integration than men – with bigger gender gaps in Britain, Ireland and Nordic countries than elsewhere. Yet we know from repeated UK polls that they are less likely to support populist Eurosceptic parties; and comparative studies also show that women are somewhat more likely to support the 'status quo' in referendums – with one theory being that women are more risk-averse.

In this respect, the Scottish referendum fitted with the general pattern of referendums across Europe: in YouGov's post-referendum poll, asking people how they had voted, 51% of men said they had voted Yes compared to only 42% of women.[2] The main obstacle for 'Leave', therefore, may be that even while women may be more sceptical than men about the EU, they remain harder to convince that they should vote to leave it.

The 'In' campaign faces a different challenge, one of mobilising women who are not particularly Eurosceptic and would be more likely to vote 'In' than 'Out' if they voted – but who may not feel that the issue matters enough to them to turn out. They may face a similar challenge with younger voters, too. For both groups, macroeconomic figures about the value to GDP, or arguments about the Norwegian model, are unlikely to convince them that EU membership, in or out, has a big impact on their everyday life. In fact, for many voters, the only way they see the EU affecting them is by allowing higher levels of immigration than they would like, through free movement.

The politics of gender are not fixed – and gender gaps have changed direction, significantly, over time in British politics. The Conservatives were the main beneficiary, across most of the post-war period, of the initial extension of suffrage to women. That pattern was reversed in the 1990s, with Labour doing better than the Conservatives. Today, there are divergent patterns among different women voters: younger women are more likely than younger men to vote left; older women are more likely than older men to vote right.

The lesson for the EU referendum of those shifting patterns is that there is no political destiny in demographics – it depends on the arguments that the campaigns make about what is at stake and why. The votes of women may be decisive in the referendum and they are up for grabs for both sides. Yet neither campaign seems to be making any kind of sustained bid to secure them.

Women's votes will be important in the election but they will not vote as a bloc. Campaigners will need to take account of differences between young and old, married and unmarried, women who are working and those without a paid job. Indeed the same is true of all groups of voters: it is widely known that young graduates will trend 'In' but how young DE voters who left school at 18 will vote is less widely understood. Voters will be influenced by a range of factors and advocates will need to build up a picture of the various 'tribes' of referendum voters, how they are likely to vote and the approaches and messengers that are most likely to persuade them.

'HAPPY FAMILIES'

ALEX

Alex knows which way he's voting – 'In'. He traveled and worked a bit in Europe during a gap year before university. He graduated a few years ago and has no particular plans to move to Europe, but he wants the option and wouldn't want it denied to others. He liked Nick Clegg's pro-European stance but ditched the Lib Dems for the Greens at the last election. He likes their liberal approach to immigration and thinks we'd be fine with more of it – since he moved to London for work, he's loved the cosmopolitan feel that comes from lots of different cultures rubbing-along together.

He argues with his Dad about supporting UKIP and while he's not one for demonstrations he has signed petitions supporting a more humane approach to immigration.

Alex would probably describe himself as more European than British. He certainly finds Englishness, with all its flag-waving, a bit worrying.

42% of those certain to vote 'In' have a university degree, compared to 28% of those certain to vote 'Out'. (ICM for British Future)

DON

Don is Alex's Dad. He and Nancy still live in Great Yarmouth, where they moved in the 1970s for work – he used to service the oil rigs. Retired now, he was made redundant about ten years ago and struggled to find work after that. He's amazed by how much the town, and the whole country, has changed in the last thirty years – the Internet, young people all going off to university. And of course immigration – every day he reads in the paper how many more are coming. We can't even deport the bad ones because of human rights. And what jobs are there going to be for the grandkids?

It seems that only Nigel Farage is talking about it – and UKIP seem to be the only ones who aren't afraid to say they're proud to be English, too. That's why he switched to UKIP at the last election – he voted for David Cameron in the previous one. He'll be voting 'Out' in the referendum for sure.

> *Twice as many over-65s (21%*
> *to 10%) say they're certain*
> *to vote 'Out' than 18 – 24-year-olds.*
> *(ICM for British Future)*

His wife **Nancy** doesn't really like politics much – you can't believe any of them and they all sound so similar– but she's not so keen on Don's UKIP. Nigel Farage and his party just seem to have a bit of a nasty edge to them, and she prefers David Cameron. She reads about all the immigrants when she picks up his paper, but she doesn't see a lot of them round the town.

Nancy's really not sure about the EU – she tends to zone out when Don goes on about it. She hasn't really considered whether she'll vote as she doesn't think she knows enough about it – though they do seem to spend a lot of our money in Brussels, and the French don't seem to be helping with all those people trying to get through the Channel Tunnel. If anything she'd probably vote 'Out', unless David Cameron can get them to change things.

One thing she does agree with Don about, though, is that the 'politically correct mob' should stop doing the country down so much.

It was great when everyone on the street got together for the Jubilee and the Olympics and hung the Union Jack out of their windows. We should all be proud to be British.

> *Women are twice as likely as men (18% to 9%) to say they don't know which way they will vote in the referendum. (ICM for British Future)*

ANNA

Anna is their daughter. Like Alex, she left Great Yarmouth pretty soon after university, when she married Stuart. They moved to Rugby about five years ago with her job, as an HR manager.

She voted for David Cameron at the election, the first time she's ever voted Conservative. She thinks they're the only ones that can be trusted with the economy – and that's why she's pleased the PM will try to keep us in Europe too. The company she works for is international and she worries they might leave if we weren't part of Europe.

Since they had a baby last year, Anna's already started worrying about getting her into a decent school and the cost of moving to a bigger house in a couple of years. She can't help thinking that immigration has got to be a factor in all of this, with lots of new people arriving here.

Half the people she works with now are from other parts of Europe. But she wants her daughter to have all the opportunities she had, and cutting Britain off from the rest of the Europe will only narrow her horizons – so she's hoping David Cameron can really get the changes to the EU that he's been talking about. If he does, she'll probably vote to stay in the EU.

Stuart, her husband, doesn't agree. He runs a small building firm that's been struggling since the influx of cheaper foreign labour from Europe. He thinks we need to get immigration down and getting out of the EU might be the only way, unless Cameron can get some kind of cap on free movement.

Stuart's always voted Conservative as the best party for small businesses. He thinks the EU have brought in a load of red tape that makes things more difficult for people like him.

When they go back to Great Yarmouth he and Don love winding-up Anna about Europe and its diktats on straight bananas. But he wouldn't vote UKIP – he wouldn't trust them to run the economy as they only seem to have any policies on immigration. He's probably voting to leave, unless we can get a much better deal from Europe.

Jason is 20 and works for Stuart in the building firm. He didn't go to university but he did a business course at college so he doesn't want to spend his whole life on building sites.

He can't see why Stuart gets so wound up by the EU. It's good that he and his mates get into the faster passport queue when they go on their summer holiday. Other than that it doesn't really affect him. It meant that Chelsea could bring in Eden Hazard last year – would we even be in the Champions League if Britain pulled out of Europe?

Jason thinks Farage is quite funny, the only politician who likes a fag and a pint. None of them really seem normal. He didn't get round to registering to vote in the election and he knows his boss is going to go on at him about it, but he can't see why he'd bother voting in the referendum.

LEE

Back in Great Yarmouth, **Lee** is one of Don's mates from the pub – they used to work together for a while too. Lee got made redundant around the same time as Don, from a job that he's had since he left school. He was unemployed for a few years before finding a part-time job for the council.

It's Lee that's trying to get Don out to do some door-knocking for UKIP. He thinks they're the only answer to the tide of immigrants that have changed the country beyond recognition. He thinks that leaving Europe – and getting rid of some of the millions who've moved here to get council houses and benefits – is the only way for white Britons to get their country back.

Nearly six in ten (58%) of certain
'Out' voters left education after
secondary school; that figure
is just 38% for certain 'In' voters.
(ICM for British Future)

Lee knocked on doors for UKIP in the last election – just like he did for the BNP when they had a candidate a couple of elections back, though there's nobody standing for them now. He doesn't care what deals David Cameron says he's got from Europe: he'd never trust a Tory and thinks Labour is a complete joke since they got taken over by Oxbridge socialists – none of them would recognize a working-class man if one fell on them.

THE WIDER FAMILY: WHO ARE THE OTHER
CHARACTERS OF THE REFERENDUM?

Siobhan is an 18-year-old Scottish student. She's newly fascinated by politics after the referendum in Scotland, which prompted her no vote 'Yes' and join the SNP. A keen believer in the party's progressive liberal values, she's strongly 'In' for the EU referendum and is certain to vote – but there's a little bit of her that hopes it all goes wrong. After all, if English votes alone take the UK out of the EU, surely they'd get another crack at an independence referendum?

Callum, Siobhan's boyfriend, is also a student and became more politically engaged since he left home, but it's tuition fees, UKUncut and Occupy that have grabbed his attention. He'd always thought he was pro-EU until Owen Jones started making a case for 'Lexit'. He thought Syriza in Greece offered a real future for the Left in Europe and after what the EU has done to them, he might angry enough to change his mind and vote 'Out'.

Freddy is, by his own admission, "an unreconstructed Thatcherite city boy". 35 years old, unattached and making bags of money, he wants an open, unregulated economy so he can make even more. Most of his colleagues don't agree, but he likes what Douglas Carswell is saying – get out from under the EU, open up Britain for global business, and let non-EU migrants in if they've got the skills: someone's got to do up his new flat in Battersea.

FIROZ

Firoz is a middle-manager in a small IT firm and is doing pretty well – so he voted Tory for the first time in 2015 as he was worried what Ed Miliband might do to the economy. A British Asian from Kent, he's patriotic and supports England *almost* as much as he loves Manchester United. He's no great fan of the EU, in part because it seems so unfair that anyone from Poland or Romania can come here, but if you're from India you need to jump all kinds of hurdles. But he's even less keen on UKIP and Nigel Farage, and some of the people in his town who support them – so if he does vote in the referendum, it will be for 'In', just so they don't win.

Two-thirds of non-white Britons say they would never vote UKIP. 65% of ethnic minority voters describe the party as 'dangerous and divisive'. (Survation for British Future)

---

3. *HOW NOT TO TALK ABOUT EUROPE –* WHY BOTH SIDES RISK HELPING THEIR OPPONENTS WIN THE REFERENDUM

It's easy talking to people who already agree with you, about topics that you're both excited about. It's no way to win a referendum, though.

Quite the opposite, in fact: by speaking passionately to fellow believers, both sides in the EU referendum risk harming their own cause, turning-off voters those whose minds are not yet fully made up. While mobilising activists may be important to the ground game, the referendum will be decided by 'don't knows', 'don't cares' and 'don't-yet-know-enough-to-decides'.

Neither 'In' nor 'Out' has yet succeeded in reaching past their base to the true battleground of the referendum debate. But a good referendum, one that reaches a satisfactory, democratic conclusion to the long-running debate on Britain's EU membership, will need to be one that engages as wide a cross-section of the public as possible.

Both sides of the debate would be wise to pay heed to some key considerations if they wish to win over undecided referendum voters.

(i) Look who's talking

Some of the most passionate advocates for both 'in' and 'out' may be popular with existing supporters, but not with those who are unsure or leaning the other way. Polling by Survation for British Future finds that the two least-trusted voices on Europe are Nigel Farage and Tony Blair – champions respectively of the 'Leave' and 'Remain' camps.

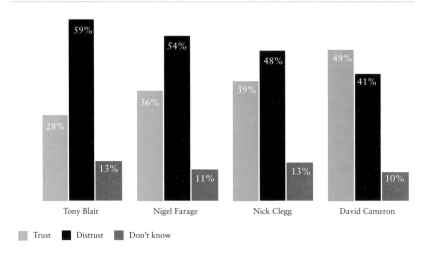

Nigel Farage's polarising language on immigration appeals strongly to those with the most negative views on the issue, but they make up only between one fifth and a quarter of the population. For many others – including those who are 'leaning out' but not fully decided – Farage and UKIP are a turn-off.

Ethnic minorities are the fastest-growing section of the UK population and made up around 10% of voters in the 2015 General Election. It is reasonable to project that they will make up around 10% of voters in the referendum too, if the respective campaigns succeed in engaging minority voters enough to ensure that they turn out to vote. This may not happen of its own accord – studies, including the recent report from the Runnymede Trust *This is still about us – Why ethnic minorities think differently about immigration* – find that BME voters feel more detached from the Europe debate than their white neighbours.[3]

Polling by Survation for British Future finds that over half of minorities (55%) feel that UKIP can fairly be described as 'racist'.

65% said they feel that UKIP's contribution to the General Election campaign was 'dangerous and divisive'. A 'leave' campaign that is very closely associated with UKIP will struggle to appeal to minorities. Yet this group should not be written-off by the 'Leave' campaign – many could be small-c conservatives and natural Eurosceptics, suspicious of the 'big government' from Brussels and favouring stronger ties to the commonwealth.

Blair may be a less polarising figure than Farage but our Survation poll finds him to be the least-trusted voice in the EU debate. Nearly six in ten people (59%) distrust the former Prime Minister when he talks about whether Britain should remain in the EU, while just 28% say they trust him on the issue. Mr Blair is even distrusted by those whose views on Britain's EU membership align closely with his own: only 42% of those who say they are definitely voting 'in' trust the former Labour PM, compared to 46% who say they distrust him.

Immigration is one area in which Blairites appear to have abandoned their 'do what works' credo for one that could be better summed up as "no compromise with the electorate". Tony Blair and his allies have responded to public anxieties about immigration by bombarding people with facts about its positive impact on GDP and "myth busting" arguments about the pressures it can bring. Yet these arguments seldom win people over who don't already agree. In fact they can make people feel more anxious and mistrustful.

For 'In', Blair's association with a previous Labour government that was perceived to be lax on spending and on immigration controls will only reinforce some of the arguments put forward by those seeking to leave the EU.

Business should also be watchful of the impact that messengers can have on the reception of its arguments to remain in the EU. Reeling-off intangible figures about GDP and telling people that the EU is good for them will mean little to people who understand the economy primarily in terms of their personal finances and job security. 'It seems to be working out very well for you' is a much more likely conclusion.

That is only made worse by the message being delivered by a corporate CEO in an expensive suit, with a view of the Square Mile from the boardroom window in the background.

Indeed, much 'In' advocacy speaks to the confident, graduate experience of the EU and has much less to say to those in a less secure economic position. It will be important for 'In' to strike a balance and offer reassurance, broadening the campaign with more blue-collar voices. Labour's Alan Johnson is a distinctive voice in this respect, as an effective communicator for 'In' who can connect with this non-graduate audience.

'In' will also need to recognize and manage the tensions between different voices that may want the same referendum result but approach the question from opposite ends. Business voices urging a reduction in 'EU bureaucracy' in the renegotiation may be speaking of EU workplace protections that trade union leaders will fight to maintain. One person's 'red tape' is another's maternity leave and paid holiday.

'Out' may face a similar challenge with less well-off voters if its answer to concerns for Britain's economy post-Brexit is that 'there may be some short-term turbulence but it will work out better in the long run'. That may make sense to some economists and the business community; for others further down the wage scale it may sound rather like 'you could be out of work'.

Painting by numbers – will voters get the picture?
'In' likes big numbers (unless they're migration figures). Europe's a big market, with lots of well-off countries, doing lots of business with each other.

What it overestimates is how much those numbers mean to the average referendum voter. British Future's 2014 pamphlet *How to talk about immigration*[4] also studied this phenomenon. Focus groups reported feeling more anxious about immigration after they had been given a series of positive statistics-based messages about the topic. They didn't believe the official statistics that were supposed to convince them of the economic benefits of immigration.

They also commit a textbook error in how *not* to have a conversation (as opposed to a lecture). What is *said* is quite different to what is *heard* by the person they're talking to. Few people understand the economy in terms of GDP or export figures; it's much more about their job, their pay and their bank balance.

If people don't believe the economy's working well for them, telling them that they're wrong and showing them a graph to prove it won't help. As Drew Weston's research in *The Political Brain*[5] shows, people can find it condescending when advocates think they have the high ground both factually and morally.

By focusing solely on facts and figures, 'In' advocates also seriously underestimate the extent to which less tangible factors, like identity and belonging, influence people's thinking about the future of their country.

DOING BRITAIN DOWN – BY TALKING EUROPE UP

Most people who live in in Britain like Britain. They're proud of their country, its history and its traditions. And while they're aware of Britain's flaws, they don't like someone else pointing them out. A failure to grasp this profound sense of pride in our identity underscores the fundamental weakness of the argument that 'Great Britain would just be Little England outside the EU'.

The UK is the world's fifth-largest economy, a permanent member of the UN Security Council with a seat at the G7. To suggest it needs the EU as much as countries with the economic and diplomatic weight of Belgium of Luxembourg is, to many, more likely to cause offence than to inspire support.

Such objective national self-criticism may be something with which metropolitan liberals feel comfortable. They may be critical of Britain's history and our colonial past and find flag-waving jingoistic and exclusive. Some may even define their identity as more European than British. But they should remember that this is a minority position. Most Britons are proud of our past and feel that how we remember and celebrate it is a big part of our contemporary identity. If Europhiles want to win over the British people, they would do well to stop sounding as if they don't like Britain.

Those advocating for the UK to stay in the EU will not benefit from appearing to think that Britain is not good or strong enough on its own. That will hand ownership of the powerful ideals of patriotism, identity and history to their opponents.

Fear is not the key

'Better Together' won the referendum on Scotland's independence – but only just. Its appeal to people's fears of the unknown if Scotland broke away may have stuck with many voters and just edged the ballot in Scotland, but it was the positive message of 'Yes' that won the campaign. 'No' started with a 20-point lead in Scotland and ended with half of that. A similar trajectory would lead to 'Leave' winning an EU referendum that is starting almost neck-and-neck.

The challenge for 'Remain' will be to make a positive pitch for the status quo.

Labour Party advocates for 'Remain' will be particularly mindful of the lessons from Scotland, where the momentum of the 'Yes' campaign carried through into the General Election and led to Labour's eradication in Scottish parliamentary seats.

But the risks of a campaign based on fear are not only relevant to those who want Britain to stay in the EU. Much of UKIP's momentum as a Eurosceptic party has been based on negative campaigning about immigration. While pollsters continue to find that most voters are concerned about this issue, UKIP hits a 'Purple ceiling' of support at around 20% – not enough to win a referendum.

The challenge for 'Leave' will be to make a positive case for a prosperous and inclusive future Britain outside the EU. While this baton has been firmly grasped by Eurosceptics Douglas Carswell MP and Dan Hannan MEP, it remains to be seen what share of public voice they have in the referendum campaign, particularly when the more negative voice of UKIP Leader Nigel Farage enjoys such a high media profile.

UKIP modernisers like Carswell face a challenge. UKIP will only break through the 15–20% 'Purple ceiling' by appealing to groups they currently fail to reach – and to do so they may need a credible, positive message on immigration. Yet such an attempt to reach out to the centre-right may alienate some of their more hardline grassroots supporters. As Nigel Farage reportedly told interviewers for *Ukip: Inside the Campaign to Redraw the Map of British Politics*, a book about the party by the academics Matthew Goodwin and Caitlin Milazzo, "The more that they know about Carswell, the less UKIP activists will like him."[6]

Embrace your own fears

Both sides in the EU referendum have their own comfort zones, topics on which they could talk for hours: for 'In' it's continuity and the economy; for 'Out' it's free movement and immigration.

But if they want to get to the parts of the electorate that their campaigns have yet to reach, both will need to get onto less comfortable territory. It's actually less a case of tackling their own fears and more one of offering reassurance to voters who have fears about them.

For 'In' this means free movement. It will not be possible for 'In' to put forward a convincing argument that net migration numbers could be reduced much below the current relatively high levels, while workers from other EU countries can come here under free movement rules. And with more than half the public listing immigration as one of their top concerns, it is not an issue that the 'In' campaign can ignore – not least because it is the one aspect of EU membership that most people see as affecting them.

Our ICM poll asked people whether they thought particular characteristics applied to the people running the 'In' and 'Out' EU referendum campaigns. Only 12% described the 'In' campaign as being 'in touch with the concerns of ordinary people', while twice as many (24%) said it was 'out of touch with ordinary people'. For 'Out', the figures are reversed, with a quarter of people saying they are in touch with people's concerns.

As we discuss in more detail in the section on immigration, a better approach for 'In' would therefore be to talk about how they propose to manage the impacts of migration levels that come with free movement, in order to secure the benefits.

The greatest fear for 'Out' is fear itself – in fact there's a decent chance it will cost them the referendum. Most commentators believe that the perceived risk of leaving the EU will be one of the chief drivers of voting to maintain the status quo. While committed Eurosceptics are convinced that Britain will thrive outside the EU – or that no scenario could be any worse than what we have at the moment – not everyone shares that confidence.

'Out' will have to tackle this and present a positive and realistic picture of a confident, prosperous and inclusive Britain outside the EU if it wants to get across the 51% finishing-line. That is not how they are perceived at the moment: twice as many people in our ICM poll say that 'Out' campaigners have a negative agenda (26%) than a positive agenda (13%).

Figure 5: What does the public think of the people running the 'In' and 'Out' campaigns?

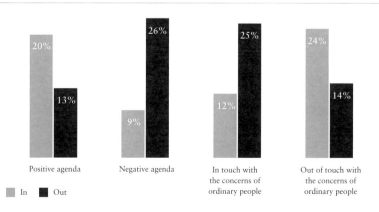

Positive agenda   Negative agenda   In touch with the concerns of ordinary people   Out of touch with the concerns of ordinary people

In   Out

PART II

SO HOW SHOULD
BOTH SIDES TALK ABOUT
EUROPE?
(AND WHAT SHOULD
THEY AVOID?)

"One camp worries about jobs, border posts and passports; the other talks passionately about national sovereignty, and hears the call of history. Europhobes are from Mars; Europhiles are from Venus."[7]
Writing in *The Guardian* on the debate about 'Brexit', John Harris notes the sharp contrast between the rational, intellectual advocacy of the pro-Europeans and the passion of their Eurosceptic opponents. He captures the challenges that both the anti- and pro-EU tribes must face up to if either of these two passionate minority groups is to secure the support of a majority of their fellow citizens in this referendum.

The challenge for 'Out' is that it cannot win on passion alone. Eurosceptics will certainly need a credible plan for what 'out' looks like, from how Britain would leave to the economic, trade and immigration plans and treaties that they would put in place. But the big question for 'Out' is not really the nuts and bolts of what Britain would look like outside the EU. Rather, it is also a question of culture and identity, of motives and trust. Could 'Out' win the trust of the majority that they are comfortable with modern Britain as it is – so that they can appeal to younger Britons, to women as well as men, and to first generation migrants and their British-born children?

> *"Will 'In' wrap itself in the blue and yellow of the EU flag, or speak powerfully to the identities that matter to most people in Britain?"*

Will 'In' prove as interested in stepping up to their challenge of reaching the centre? They are looking through the other end of the telescope. Detailed scrutiny will not be enough. The 'In' side has no end of questions to ask about whether the sums add up, with its facts and figures about the economy and trade, with statistics about the net contribution of migrants and warnings about the economic risks of exit. That case for 'In' will do well enough for most Liberal Democrats and carry a clear majority of graduates in all of the big cities. It will hold on to anybody who is already certain to vote to stay in.

The problem is that the pro-EU camp is struggling to be heard by anybody who doesn't already agree. The question for the 'In' campaign is whether it wants to run a nit-picking campaign, where its only emotional argument is the fear of exit. Doing so would concede the passion and the patriotism, the claims to history and identity, to their opponent. Do that, and an EU referendum campaign which looks like the Lib Dem EU election "party of in" pitch, or the case for electoral reform that got hammered in the Alternative Vote referendum, will quite probably lose an argument that could have been won. The challenge for pro-Europeans is whether they can argue their case with passion as well as reason: will 'In' wrap itself in the blue and yellow of the EU flag, or speak powerfully to the identities that matter to most people in Britain?

Whichever side can meet these challenges may be on the way to reaching out beyond their own tribe to secure the majority support that they need.

4. *THIS SCEPTRED ISLE:* HOW TO TALK TO THE BRITISH ABOUT IDENTITY

When people head to the polling booths in 2016 or 2017 to cast their ballots in the referendum, they will not be making a decision about Europe, but a decision about Britain.

This may sound like a statement of the obvious, but it contains an important message for the two sides campaigning for those votes. Whether you are 'In' or 'Out', if you want to talk to voters about Britain and Europe, you need to have an account of Britain that people recognise and embrace.

This is not, after all, a battle between European and British identities. Were that the case, there would be a landslide decision to leave. Most people in Britain do not feel distinctively 'European': only 4% of people in England and 2% in Scotland chose it to describe their primary identity in NatCen's 2014 *British Social Attitudes* survey.

Figure 6: British, Scottish and English identity vs European identity

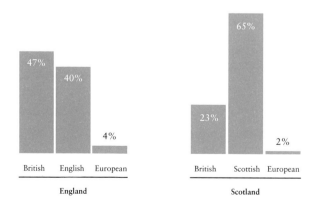

Source: NatCen's British Social Attitudes 2014

Those seeking to persuade people about the referendum choice also need a convincing account of who we think we are, what our history means today, and how that should shape our future choices. The British choice to join Europe was transactional – primarily about joining an economic club for economic reasons. We talk about Europe partly in terms of a pragmatic calculus of gains and costs, what we put in and what we get out. But our debate about Europe has always been an argument about identity too.

WHY IS BRITAIN DIFFERENT? THE ROOTS OF BRITISH EXCEPTIONALISM

The British see Europe differently – and are seen as rather reluctant Europeans by others too. Ideas of our exceptionalism are often traced a long way back: to Magna Carta; to Henry VIII breaking with Rome; and from the geographical fact of our island nation and how much that has meant for the national imagination from Shakespeare to Churchill and beyond.

Curiously, it was France's greatest President who offered the most eloquent account of British exceptionalism, albeit casually conflating England and Britain. Explaining his 1963 veto of British membership of the EEC, General de Gaulle described us thus:

"England in effect is insular, she is maritime, she is linked through her exchanges, her markets, her supply lines to the most diverse and often the most distant countries; she pursues essentially industrial and commercial activities, and only slight agricultural ones. She has in all her doings very marked and very original habits and traditions. In short, the nature, the structure, the very conjuncture that are England's differ profoundly from those of the continentals."[8]

De Gaulle's famous *non* shows how Britain's union with Europe was, from the start, a reluctant one for both parties. Having initially been in favour of Europe as a fine project for *other* Europeans, while Britain stayed at the top table with bigger fish to fry alongside the

US and the Soviets, Britain found itself adjusting to its post-Suez loss of great power status at the same time as wondering why a nation which had won the war was, within a single generation, already struggling to *catch-up* economically with those who had been on the losing side.

So post-war Britain had a rather different 'psychological contract' with the European project than our partners, most of whom gained something positive in their national narrative by making their own choices for Europe. For France, Germany and the core Benelux countries, European cooperation was founded in their 'never again' compact after seventy years of recurring conflict. Our nearest neighbour Ireland saw Europe as a way to move beyond England's shadow, reimagining itself as a younger, modernizing, more confident country. For Spain, Portugal and Greece, joining Europe meant "modernity" and another way to entrench democracy when the dictatorships fell as late as the 1970s, just as the central and East European countries saw EU membership as completing the dissolution of the iron curtain which had isolated them from the other half of the continent.

The British decision to join coincided with the nadir of national self-confidence. The 1975 referendum campaign saw the public asked, a couple of years after the event, not whether to join, but whether they wanted to stay in. It was summed up by Sir Christopher Soames warning that "in our present, parlous condition, this is no time for Britain to consider leaving a Christmas club, let alone the Common market."

That era of decline has long been over – but neither side of the European debate has entirely moved on from it.

WHY THE OLD CASE FOR EUROPE MAKES A LOSING ARGUMENT TO BRITAIN

'This is the story of fifty years in which Britain struggled to reconcile the history she could not forget with the future she could not avoid' – Hugo Young.[9]

In one sentence, the opening line of Hugo Young's *This Blessed Plot* encapsulates the core of the traditional pro-European narrative about Britain's troubled relationship with Europe.

Young's book is an elegant lament for the opportunities lost, concluding that Britain must finally realise the value of choosing to be at the heart of Europe if we are to shape a European project more to British tastes.

That narrative has underpinned the public arguments of at least three generations of pro-European British politicians. The thread runs from the Ted Heath and Roy Jenkins generation which eventually took Britain in; the Ken Clarke and Michael Heseltine pro-EU Tories who fought a bitter battle with Eurosceptics in the Thatcher and Major years; and those like Tony Blair, Peter Mandelson and Nick Clegg who also voiced ambitions to end Britain's history of ambiguity, yet remained trapped within it. But it does not offer good foundations for making an effective case.

Young's opening sentence exemplifies three ways in which this traditional pro-European narrative struggles to connect with how the British think about identity and the Europe debate.

Firstly, it posits Britain's European destiny as unavoidable – that there is no alternative. The fact of the forthcoming referendum underlines how this can no longer simply be asserted as self-evident and incontestable. An argument for *this* future must be won, over other alternative, competing choices.

> *"It might be difficult, anywhere, to win an argument about the future by telling people to become less attached to their history. There is perhaps nowhere this would be quite so true as in Britain."*

Secondly, Young identifies Britain's sense of history as a barrier to the future we should want. Pejorative metaphors about historical hangovers, post-imperial baggage weighing us down and nostalgic blinkers preventing us seeing where our modern interests now lie have been a staple of pro-European speeches. It might be difficult, anywhere, to win an argument about the future by telling people to become less attached to their history. There is perhaps nowhere this would be quite so true as in Britain. The rise in popular history, on television, in the bookshops, in museums, in the enormous public response to the Tower of London poppies and the broader First World War centenary commemorations, suggest a society becoming ever more interested in understanding our past, rather than moving on from it.

> *"Telling Britain it needs to think of itself as more like Belgium is probably not a winning referendum slogan for the 'In' campaign."*

So whenever the pro-European case is pitched as a chance to *escape* from this strong sense of history, rather than as embodying and continuing it, it will find itself on the wrong side of how most people think and, more pertinently, feel about history and identity – about how our sense of the past might be connected to our present and future.

Thirdly, it suggests that what needs to change is British identity and the British attitude to Europe, rather than the imperfect European Union of which we are part. Pro-Europeans risk sounding as if they think we would be more normal, and better Europeans, if only we could feel a little bit *less British*.

It was a former Belgian prime minister, Théo Lefevre, who said in 1994 that "In Europe, there are now only small countries – those that know it and those that don't know it yet". This may resonate with politicians and commentators in other European capitals and with a liberal British niche of loyal Lib Dem voters and other committed pro-Europeans. But telling Britain it needs to think of itself as more like Belgium is probably not a winning referendum slogan for the 'In' campaign.

The fatal error – of presenting a positive case for their preferred European future in the form of a negative case about Britain – is not, however, the sole preserve of the 'In' campaign. Their opponents, in a different way, commit the same blunder.

THE CHALLENGE FOR 'OUT': LEAVING 'BRING BACKERY' BEHIND

'Britain is no longer a sovereign nation. At midnight last night, we ceased to be an independent state, bound by international treaties to other independent states, and became instead a subordinate unit within a European state' – Daniel Hannan MEP.[10]

The Eurosceptic side of the argument has a good deal of confidence in how it talks about history, democracy and sovereignty. Yet it has a problem with the politics of identity too. A potent emotional cocktail of betrayal and conspiracy has been a source of much Eurosceptic passion and energy. This casts Ted Heath as a traitor, never to be forgiven, and each of his successors from Harold Wilson to David Cameron, part of an elite conspiracy of sovereignty surrendered, borders opened and Britain abolished.

It is this sense of existential pessimism that cuts Brexit campaigners off from the way most people think about the identity of Britain today.

Many people, including those who are not enamoured of the European Commission in Brussels, do not think Britain has been abolished. The core anti-Europeans risk accusing everybody else of what the Marxists used to call 'false consciousness': we might *imagine* that we are a country, and a democracy, which elects our MPs and our governments – but that is because too many of us haven't noticed that this is now a mirage. On social media, memes compare the EU to the USSR, as if Brussels were our very own Kremlin.

Whatever the pros and cons of getting out of the EU, this hyperbole just doesn't make sense to most of us. We don't think the General Elections since we joined Europe, which decided whether or not Margaret Thatcher came to power, or the rise and fall of New Labour, or whether it will be Jeremy Corbyn, George Osborne or Theresa May that occupies No 10 next, make no difference. And whether people agreed or disagreed with the decisions, the votes in the House of Commons on Nigel Lawson's budgets, the Iraq war, university tuition fees or gay marriage were important moments that made a difference to our society and our history. The idea that there are no democracies in Europe if there is political and public support for EU membership is nonsense.

"There could be no 'Leave' victory without a stronger appeal to those sections of society – notably the middle-classes and the under-40s – who are clear that they prefer modern Britain."

More broadly, there can be no 'Leave' victory without breaking the link between Brexit and 'bring backery'. Almost everybody knows that many of the ways in which British society has changed over the last half century are irreversible and here to stay. Where people do differ is in whether they would be tempted to turn back the clock should such a magic wand be available. Strikingly, one YouGov poll found almost a dead heat over whether people would turn the clock back twenty to thirty years if they could – a 39%

to 38% preference for modern Britain over the 80s or 90s. UKIP voters preferred the idea of the past by more than four to one, while Conservatives, Liberal Democrats and Labour voters all favoured modern Britain.[11]

This creates a reputational problem for the 'Leave' campaign – and a dilemma too. That powerful sense of nostalgia has driven Eurosceptic advocacy and fired up its activist base; but there could be no 'Leave' victory without a stronger appeal to those sections of society – notably the middle-classes and the under-40s – who are clear that they prefer modern Britain.

How and whether this is resolved will determine which version of the 'Leave' campaign turns up to fight this referendum. The strategic logic is to make the optimistic, outward-looking case about the future – but that might not be easy. The 'Leave' campaign needs to secure an unusually broad coalition, from the 'left behind' voters who would like to turn back the clock, to those who seek to charge ahead into a bright new global free market future.

THE IDENTITY CHALLENGES FOR 'IN' AND 'OUT'

Both competing referendum campaigns have identity challenges to overcome if they want to be confident of securing the support of more than half of Britons.

Pro-Europeans are struggling to work out whether they have a positive case to make. They may retreat to countering emotional arguments about who we are with a primarily pragmatic focus on pounds, pence and the practical risks of leaving. Europhiles are caught in a conflict – anxious that the Scottish referendum suggested that a campaign focused only on risks is too narrow, yet worried that any pro-European campaign will not have much reach and resonance beyond the already converted.

In part, this difficulty in finding a positive case arises from a category error. Pro-EU campaigners are trying to think of a positive case "for Europe" and struggle to identify one with the broad, popular potential to reach most people. What they need – and have been missing – is a positive case *about Britain*, an account of why it makes sense in terms of British history and British identity to stay in the EU.

Our sense of identity is shaped by our understanding of history. If 'In' sets out its European future in implied opposition to British history, suggesting that we must shrug off the latter to embrace the former, it will find little favour with the voting public. Rather, the 'In' campaign should seek to occupy the very territory that 'Out' considers its home turf – competing for association with the emotional symbols of these islands' history. Britain did not, after all, turn its back on the problems of its European neighbours in the two great wars by which we largely define ourselves.

It would be a mistake, however, to focus only on British identity. Among many of those whom 'In' needs to reach, the most popular identity is English – but pro-Europeans have almost nothing to say about England, except to insult it by declaring that we should want to be 'Great Britain, not Little England'. Many pro-Europeans are unaware of this, partly because they are more likely to be among those who feel more British than English – a more popular answer among Londoners, liberal-minded graduates, Liberal Democrats and ethnic minorities. This leaves pro-Europeans thinking English identity doesn't matter to people – because it doesn't matter much to them. Expecting pro-Europeans to embrace English identity, when they already struggle with Britishness, may be asking too much. But the 'In' campaign won't be speaking about the identity that matters most to many people in Britain until they do.

Eurosceptics need to show that they like and understand modern Britain. They could start by dropping an argument that really shows their age, 'we only voted for a Common Market'. This only makes sense to those with an adult memory of 1975 – and the 'Leave' campaign needs to focus on the voters who hadn't even been born then. While Brexit campaigners tend to be older, the campaign needs to find ways to reach colleges and universities if it is to attract the support of over 50% of referendum voters.

> *"Since the last EU referendum,*
> *Britain has changed considerably.*
> *Many of the voters taking*
> *part in the referendum will be part*
> *of that change."*

Since the last EU referendum, Britain has changed considerably. Many of the voters taking part in the referendum will be part of that change. It will do 'Out' no favours at all if it appears that they would rather that hadn't happened. About 10% of the British electorate is now non-white, rising to one in five first time voters. Ethnic minority votes could therefore be crucial in a close referendum. Indeed, in a hypothetical scenario where one campaign had to write ethnic minority voters off entirely, the 50% referendum threshold would rise to a need for around 56% of white British voters, while their opponents could secure a referendum victory with just 45% of the white British vote plus their ethnic minority support.

The 'Leave' campaign has considerable untapped potential with ethnic minority voters, but starts with a big reputational barrier. Many ethnic minority Britons could be natural Eurosceptic target voters: they have a stronger than average attachment to being British, and many have practical and emotional ties to the Commonwealth. But there is a major barrier of mistrust. The most prominent anti-EU voices have been toxic – with most ethnic minority voters mistrusting UKIP's claim to be an inclusive, mainstream party to the extent that a majority of non-white voters believe it is fair to characterise UKIP as 'racist'.

Some liberal Eurosceptics have recognised this challenge. UKIP MP Douglas Carswell has argued for a 'Clause Four'-style break with the Enoch Powell legacy[12] using his acceptance speech on being re-elected as UKIP to make a point of welcoming first and second generation Britons as much as any other. But the 'Leave' campaign has a lot more work to do to persuade non-white voters that it really is sincere about being an inclusive voice with a global vision of the future, not one that hankers back to the much less diverse Britain of 1950.

One rather counterintuitive way in which 'Leave' might stake just such a claim to be in touch with modern Britain is to make a positive case for Europe in Britain, if not Britain in Europe.

In some ways, the British have become somewhat more European over the last forty years. Levels of personal contact with continental Europe have grown, along with Europe's cultural presence in British society. While European food, football and cheap flights have done little to mitigate sceptical attitudes about the politics of Europe or the institutions of the European Union, they have become part of our cultural furniture. And they would remain so if Britain were to leave the EU.

The 'Leave' campaign might therefore consider challenging the idea that our sense of everyday Europe is in jeopardy. Whichever way the referendum goes, nobody doubts that there would still be baguettes and cappuccinos on the high street, stag weekends in Dublin or Prague and European football managers leading British teams into the Champions League. A campaign could critique the rules and regulations and the costs of the Common Agricultural Policy while arguing that little from Europe that makes life in Britain better is at risk in this referendum.

These simple and everyday things may represent the entirety of what Europe means to many voters. That is a very different starting point to that of the advocates, for both 'In' or 'Out', who are seeking their support. Indeed, one of the core challenges when talking about identity, for campaigners on both sides of the referendum debate, is that they may hold rather strong identities themselves – as proud Europeans or equally-proud Eurosceptics. For the majority of voters, however, Europe and the EU may have very little bearing on the identity they hold. They are more likely to consider themselves simply as British, or English, Scottish or Welsh.

WOULD BREXIT END BRITAIN? A TALE OF TWO UNIONS

For over half a century, this has been a debate about Britain and Europe. Yet British identity has changed in a changing Britain – and neither side of the EU debate has kept up.

The 'Stronger In' campaign to remain in the EU launched in red, white and blue, keen to show it is making a patriotic British case. It will need to show it can speak to Wales, Scotland and England too. UKIP's name captures that is a pro-Union British party, though Euroscepticism appeals most strongly to those who feel English rather than British. That gives the 'Leave' campaign a challenge to show it can win votes across the United Kingdom – with a particular headache over how to persuade Scotland and the consequences if it failed to do so but did win the argument elsewhere.

Strikingly, Scotland was more Eurosceptic than the rest of Britain in 1975, when 42% of Scots voted to leave, compared to 37% in Wales and just 31% in England. Northern Ireland was most Eurosceptic of all, staying in by just 48% to 52%.

Today, Scotland is consistently a bit more pro-European than England – which creates the possibility that the different UK nations might have opposing majorities for 'Remain' or for 'Leave'. The SNP argues that a Brexit vote should only be valid with an out-and-out majority in each of the four UK nations, though the referendum rules will mean that a simple UK-wide majority wins. However, clashing majorities in Scotland and the rest of Britain would be likely to trigger a new referendum on independence, a central question in Scottish politics.

Scottish pro-EU votes could, in theory, overturn a Brexit majority elsewhere in the UK if the vote was on a knife-edge. Relative population sizes means only an English 'Remain' vote of around 49% could be pushed over the line by pluralities elsewhere. With a Scottish electorate of 4 million, a much wider margin of Scots voting to stay in the EU could find their votes outweighed by Welsh and English votes to Leave. In that event, the EU referendum could well prove decisive for two Unions rather than one.

There is little evidence that many English, Welsh or Northern Irish voters would change their minds on the EU to keep the UK together. Even if majorities across the UK had hoped for a Scottish 'No' in the final weeks of the 2014 independence referendum, this is unlikely to have mass public salience during the argument about Europe. It could well be a considerably greater dilemma for Scottish Eurosceptics who support the Union.

The 'Leave' campaign should give a high priority to trying to win in Scotland as well as England. But this requires a significant cultural shift – and new messengers. Scottish attitudes towards the EU are only mildly more positive – but the reputation of UKIP is considerably more toxic in Scotland than elsewhere. The party secured just 1.6% of the General Election vote in Scotland compared to 14% in England and Wales. Research for our post-election report *The politics of immigration* found that two-thirds of Scots consider UKIP to be a 'dangerous and divisive party' which 'risks bringing prejudice into debates about immigration'.[13] This makes the cultural challenge for 'Leave' of finding a different tone and different messengers especially pressing in Scotland.

If 'Leave' won, but lost Scotland, some on the 'Out' side would find a result that was not quite the 'full Brexit'. Speaking at a British Future event, UKIP MP Douglas Carswell took an agnostic view of the future of the UK: "If I was in Scotland, I don't know how I would vote on the UK," he said, voicing an instinctive sympathy that might lie with pro-independence Scots. "Do we think it would be better if Ireland were still run from Whitehall? I'm a localist. But I'm not a Scot," he said. "Where I can be much more certain of my views is in the need to leave the EU," he added, suggesting the break-up of the UK would be a price worth paying for departure from the EU.[14]

THE AFTERMATH

In a second independence referendum, caused by Scotland being outvoted on the EU, it is widely assumed that the pro-independence side would start as favourites. However, the outcome would not be certain. This scenario would create several new questions in a fresh independence referendum: as to how Scotland could now seek to rejoin the EU, or remain a member if it could become independent before the UK's exit was formalised; about what economic relationships an independent Scotland inside the EU would have with a UK that was leaving, and whether the currency of an independent Scotland in this scenario would be the pound, the Euro or an independent Scottish currency; and about whether EU free movement and the absence of immigration controls within Britain were compatible.

There would be pressure to hold a Scottish vote relatively quickly, since it would be more difficult to negotiate the terms of exit if there was considerable uncertainty about whether Scotland would be in either the UK or the EU within a year or two.

Negotiating a British exit from the European Union is a complex task – and a British government could find itself trying to conduct departure talks from the EU and negotiations to dissolve the UK with an independent Scotland simultaneously. If Scotland had voted for the EU, and for independence, then the Scottish government would be establishing the terms of independence while also dealing with the unique situation of seeking to secure EU membership as a current part of a departing member state.

If the EU vote does lead to the dissolution of two Unions, then the British and Scottish governments would probably face the most complex diplomatic challenge of any modern democratic government – making it harder still to confidently define the consequences of a vote to leave the EU.

5. *THEY COME OVER HERE...* HOW TO TALK ABOUT IMMIGRATION AND THE EU REFERENDUM

The question "How does the EU affect you?" remains a pretty obscure one to most people – but those who can come up with an answer are most likely to say "immigration."

Immigration is bound to be an important part of the referendum campaign. Some believe it could be the dominant issue – and that it could decide the result too.

Almost three-quarters of those with strongly anti-migration views plan to vote out, while only a quarter of those who see immigration as broadly positive want Britain to leave the EU.

Among the clearest indicators of which way people will vote in the EU referendum is their attitude to immigration. An ICM poll for British Future asked people to rate the impact of immigration on the UK from 0–10, with 0 very negative and 10 very positive.

Around three-quarters of those who give immigration a score of three out of 10 or lower plan to vote 'Out' in the referendum, while only a quarter of those who see immigration as a positive (scoring it 8+ out of 10) currently want Britain to leave the EU.

Half of the country is in neither of those groups. They are the 'anxious middle' – scoring immigration between 4 and 7 out of ten, and seeing both pressures and benefits from immigration to Britain. This group is split down the middle on the EU. In British Future's ICM poll, the anxious middle split 44% for 'In' and 44% for 'Out' – and two-thirds of this group said that they could change their minds about their referendum vote.

Whether it's 'In' or 'Out', whichever campaign reaches and persuades the anxious middle is highly likely to win the referendum.

Figure 7: How EU referendum voting intention corresponds with views on immigration

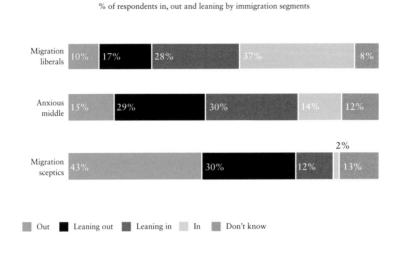

% of respondents in, out and leaning by immigration segments

| | | Out | Leaning out | Leaning in | In | Don't know |

It is fair to say that the main reason we are having this referendum is, in a word, immigration. The issue is a considerably more salient and important one to the public than the EU itself. That wasn't true in the 1990s during the debates on the Maastricht Treaty, when calls for a referendum were made but resisted. It was immigration, much more than Euroscepticism, that drove UKIP's first place in the European Elections of 2014 and their 3.8 million votes in May's General Election.

Figure 8: Ipsos MORI Issues index – immigration vs EU

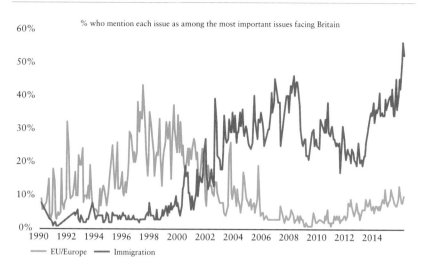

Ipsos MORI Issues Index, 1974–2014

Campaigners for staying in the EU fear that immigration could be their Achilles' heel. It is probably the main issue that they wish they didn't have to talk about. Many of those committed to campaigning for the UK to stay in Europe do see EU free movement as one of the achievements and benefits of the European Union – but pro-Europeans often lack confidence in their ability to persuade a majority of the country to see it that way.

Yet curiously, if the 'Remain' campaign struggles to find its voice on immigration, 'Leave' strategists also fear that immigration may prove to be less their trump card than their biggest dilemma. They know that immigration will motivate significant numbers of people to vote to leave – but it could prove to be the issue that toxifies their pitch too. If people feel that the case for exit is all about immigration, with little to say about anything else, then 'Leave' will be all but guaranteed to fall short of the winning post.

So it may transpire that neither side wants a referendum that is all about immigration. Equally, however, neither side will be able to duck the issue entirely or avoid its playing a significant role in how Britain decides on our membership of the EU. And whether or not immigration turns out to be the issue that does most to determine the outcome of the vote, the EU referendum result could do much to determine the future of immigration policy in Britain.

WHAT PRO-EUROPEANS GET WRONG

The 'In' campaign has three big problems on immigration.

Firstly, immigration is among the top two concerns, after sovereignty, for those who are certain they want the UK to leave the EU.

Secondly, perhaps more importantly, it is also among the top two concerns of those who are undecided – so it is one of the key issues that the public prioritises in David Cameron's reform negotiations with other EU partners.

"Many pro-Europeans wish they could talk about something else when the issue of immigration comes up. "

Thirdly, most things that most pro-Europeans instinctively feel they should say about immigration to try to persuade people may make this worse. Their response to the issue is, in most cases, more likely to harm their own cause, winning voters not for 'In', but for their rivals in the 'Out' campaign.

So it isn't surprising that many pro-Europeans wish they could talk about something else when the issue of immigration comes up. The reason the pro-EU side's arguments don't work, however, isn't for the reason that pro-Europeans tend to imagine. The problem is not that the public have hostile, hardline and impossible-to-engage-with views against immigration. They don't. It is rather that the pro-EU side haven't yet found a way to engage on immigration that preaches beyond the already converted.

Instead, they resort to a series of arguments that can be shown to be ineffective. There is a tendency to engage in "myth-busting", despite all the evidence that this fails: simple, straightforward-sounding 'myths' are remembered and reinforced while their complex explanations are forgotten. It suggests that the pro-EU side is complacent and doesn't think there is anything to sort out, except to dismiss public concerns.

'They pay in more than they take out,' the story of net contribution, is true. But it is also abstract, obscure and transactional. Research shows it is an ineffective argument that leaves the public cold. After all, if the public is concerned how well migration is managed, and whether migrants contribute and integrate, then it is curious to think that *aggregate net contribution* is the thing they would be concerned about. Those who are already sceptical about immigration will disbelieve the figures, perhaps noting they only refer to those migrants that the Government knows about. It may also underline their desire for greater selectivity in our immigration system – if net contribution is so important, why can't we just accept those migrants who contribute most?

'We can go there too' is another argument that sounds to pro-migration voices like it should work, but which fails with those who are not already onside. It is an argument that appeals primarily to the more mobile, the younger and the more cosmopolitan-minded: the profile of a likely 'In' voter. It is highly unlikely that those who want to leave the EU haven't realised that they could up sticks and move to Germany if they wanted to. It is because the option is unattractive or seen to be unachievable for all but a university-educated elite.

THE 'OUT' SIDE'S PROBLEM ON IMMIGRATION

How much to talk about immigration is the issue that divides those who want to leave the EU more than any other single issue.

UKIP leader Nigel Farage believes that the referendum can and should be won on immigration – "I have said that the key issue will be immigration, open borders and control,"[15] he has said. The UKIP leader has argued that those who want to downplay the issue are failing to play their trump card.

Other advocates for an EU exit see it differently. UKIP's only MP Douglas Carswell was among the first to warn against what he calls 'angry nativism,' as a turn-off to most voters. Other voices arguing for Brexit have made a similar point: Nigel Lawson took up a role for Conservatives for Britain, saying that his motive was to prevent "less moderate, xenophobic voices" dominating the case for exit.

Tactically, this also reflects a view that the most anti-EU and anti-immigration voters – often committed UKIP partisans – will have a high degree of motivation to turn out in an EU referendum anyway. In this respect the challenge for 'Out' is the same as that for 'In' – to reach undecided voters.

There are several signs that the official 'Out' campaign will seek to moderate its voice on immigration to try to achieve that. This reflects the evidence of what the 'anxious middle' thinks about immigration.

Dominic Cummings, former special adviser to Michael Gove and a key strategist for the 'Leave' campaign, has written that "The official OUT campaign does *not* need to focus on immigration," on the twin grounds that those angry about immigration are already motivated to vote to leave the EU, while "focusing on it would alienate other crucial parts of the electorate."[16]

For 'Out', however, the question of immigration and the referendum has to go deeper than just thinking about its tone of voice and campaign strategy. The 'anxious middle' voters will also want to know what leaving the European Union will or won't mean for

Britain's future choices about immigration. That debate has yet to progress beyond soundbites – but the voters will expect a clearer plan than that.

The 'Australian points system' is a popular slogan that resonates with voters – because it is shorthand for a controlled and selective migration policy, which does welcome those with skills we need and suggests an Aussie 'toughness' towards the unskilled. But the slogan is a long way from stacking up as a policy for Britain – a country with a very different geography, demography and set of regional economic relationships to Australia. Indeed, take calls for emulating the antipodean approach to immigration seriously, in policy terms, and this would lead to a significant *increase* in immigration to Britain, not a reduction at all. Net migration to Australia is 260,000 a year in a country with a population of just 19 million people. Relative to population, immigration to Australia is three times as high as that to the UK.

> *"The unanswered question here is whether it is possible to negotiate a free trade deal which does not include free movement."*

So 'Out' has to answer three important questions about what, if anything, would change about immigration when Britain left the EU.

Firstly, would leaving the EU actually lead to significant changes to free movement? This is widely asserted to be a significant part of the argument for 'Out' – but the unanswered question here is whether it is possible to negotiate a free trade deal which does not include free movement. At present, those non-EU members with free trade access, such as Norway and Switzerland, are part of free movement under that free trade deal. If the priority is to end free movement, a different deal would be necessary – or Britain could give priority to ending free movement over free trade access.

It is going to be very difficult to answer this question definitively before a referendum, because the answer will depend on the negotiations that take place afterwards. What voters *can* reasonably ask, however, ıs this: what is the most important priority for a post-Brexit Britain? At present, it is sensible to assume that a guarantee of free trade access would probably mean a willingness to accept the continuation of free movement, at least for a significant period, while a commitment to end free movement would mean a willingness to accept limitations on trade access. To change that, 'Leave' campaigners would need to produce a clear and workable plan for post-EU immigration policy, and show persuasively that it would be an achievable deal that other EU members would see as being in their interests.

Secondly, what would happen to EU citizens already in the UK? This became a point of controversy during the Rochester by-election when Mark Reckless, seeking to be re-elected after switching from the Conservatives to UKIP, talked about repatriation. UKIP then changed its position to argue that all Europeans here legally before the referendum would have the right to remain and to apply for British citizenship. UKIP MP Douglas Carswell, who grew up in Uganda, has said that to do anything else would have echoes of Idi Amin. That position is endorsed by Labour Eurosceptics such as Graham Stringer MP.

Nigel Farage has spoken of 'sensible reciprocal arrangements' – but it is very difficult to find any plan from any Eurosceptic voice about what form these would take. Most of the British public will recognise that it won't be possible to retain the rights of Britons to work in the EU while removing the rights of Europeans to work in Britain. An approach where the UK has free movement with 'old Europe' but not with Central and Eastern Europe might well chime with British public opinion, but it is impossible to imagine EU members, whether Germany or Poland, offering such a 'pick and mix' deal to a departing member.

Thirdly, what would leaving the EU mean for non-EU immigration? 'Out' campaigners have suggested that moving away from free movement, should that prove viable, would allow a more generous approach to non-EU migrants. This can be an attractive position, one that speaks to the public's desire for selectivity and skills to be a central factor when deciding who can settle in the UK. By speaking positively about Indian migrants, 'Out' voices also hope to address the reputational problems for Brexit campaigners arising from UKIP's negative reputation among younger and more liberal voters. Such proposals aim to shift what is currently a toxic reputation with a majority of Asian and black voters, who could find some appeal in an argument to rebalance European and Commonwealth migration, if they were to trust the motives of the messenger.

So this is a politically attractive proposal for Leave – but there is also a clear policy consequence of making it. The idea that Brexit makes greater generosity to non-EU migrants possible is a coherent position if and only if those making it acknowledge that leaving the EU would not, therefore, make it possible to reduce net migration levels to anything like the government's 'tens of thousands' target. After all, non-EU net migration is 201,000[17] – so the laws of mathematics are clear that you can't put this number up and achieve a reduction to the 'tens of thousands'. If, on the other hand, the 'Out' campaign wants to argue for an immigration policy that would significantly reduce overall net migration numbers to the kind of level aspired to by Home Secretary Theresa May, an honest campaign would have to argue for more restrictive non-EU migration – not a more welcoming approach to skilled Indians and Commonwealth migrants.

YOU CAN'T ALWAYS GET WHAT YOU WANT

What the general public, especially the anxious middle, might ideally want is not going to be on offer from either side in this referendum. Selective immigration based on skills, from inside as well as outside the EU, but without having to leave the club to get it, is not an offer that either side can put on the table.

Instead of pretending that it is, both sides need to set out a real-world vision of what immigration would look like if they win the referendum. Pro-EU voices will need to set out a plan for what they *can* do to manage relatively-high levels of migration better. Eurosceptic voices who are serious about winning need to move on, from highlighting what they don't like, to a convincing argument about what could change if we left.

"Both sides need to set out a real-world vision of what immigration would look like if they win the referendum."

The Prime Minister's focus has been on changing the welfare rules for migrants, so that EU migrants are only eligible for in-work or out-of-work benefits after a qualifying period. He has proposed this should be four years. There is little doubt that this would be popular with the British public if it could be delivered: our research has found that is the change to EU immigration that the public would most like.

A compromise on the details could find favour too. Indeed, the British Social Attitudes survey[18] shows public opinion to be mildly softer than the government's proposal: 61% of people would favour EU migrants having full and equal access after three years, while a significant minority (37%) favour a delay of just one year. Only 18%

of people say EU migrants should wait five years or longer for equal access, while only 1% say EU citizens should never gain the same welfare rights as British citizens. This shows that most people do see welfare access as a club, where people do need to earn entitlements, but also that they should then have equal status within the club that they have joined.

The reform may be difficult to achieve because of political objections from other EU leaders or legal rules against discriminating against EU nationals from other countries. It may be that a political deal between governments could find a formula to resolve this. Otherwise, the main route to changing the welfare rules for EU migrants would depend on a more far-reaching reform of British welfare, towards a more contributory system, affecting UK and EU citizens alike. That has become an increasingly important theme in the UK welfare debate, but would be a much bigger reform agenda than the referendum timetable allows. The Foreign Secretary has suggested that, if the welfare changes that the government is seeking don't prove possible, the British government could argue for "quantitative controls" – limits on the numbers of EU migrants allowed in – instead. But he also acknowledged that other EU governments would find that harder to agree to.

There is another problem with David Cameron's approach – beyond how much of his proposed reform he can get – which is the government's argument about what would result from it. The new rules could be sold effectively as a response to public concerns that those who come to Britain are here for the right reasons; it is less clear that a claim that such changes would significantly reduce the levels of EU migration is credible.

EU migrants would be less well-off in their first years in Britain, if unable to claim tax credits, but that would not negate several other attractions of Britain for those who come here to work. The Polish migrants who took part in British Future's Southampton research spoke of their experience of Britain being a place where those seeking work could find it – saying they could not see how anybody could look for work for six months and not succeed – and often spoke about how and why they had taken entry level jobs for which they were over-qualified, because they saw Britain as a country where promotion and progression in the workplace were possible for those who work hard. A growing economy and the English language are positive features of the UK that can't be changed for EU migrants alone.

> *"If achieved, welfare reforms could have a moderate impact on immigration numbers, but there is little to suggest this would be transformative."*

If achieved, welfare reforms could have a moderate impact on immigration numbers, but there is little to suggest this would be transformative. Cynics might suggest that the referendum will take place before voters find out what the actual impact has been. That risks underestimating how far previous failed predictions and promises have eroded public trust – first, with the Labour government wrongly anticipating fairly low levels of immigration from Poland after 2004, and then with the Conservative promise to bring immigration numbers down, before seeing them go up instead.

There is little realistic prospect that the government's EU reform proposals, if agreed, would reduce EU migration by many tens of thousands. Yet that is what would be needed for there to be any real-world prospect of the government having a chance of fulfilling its ambition to get overall net migration below 100,000.

Those advocating that we stay in the EU should acknowledge the reality that it will not be possible to make any firm pledges on

EU immigration numbers while Britain remains in the club. Remaining in the EU means a higher level of unskilled migration than people would ideally want. The detail of EU negotiations could perhaps lead to new offers that can be made about future arrangements too, such as maintaining seven-year transitional periods for new members like Croatia, or making the highly hypothetical future accession of Turkey conditional on different arrangements. But none of this would significantly cut the current levels of EU migration. A more effective defence of free movement can't just involve symbolic reassurances about future scenarios: it needs to focus much more on practical plans to handle migration better.

The main argument of the 'In' campaign to date has been to argue that free movement is part and parcel of free trade. That could allow them to question whether or not these rules would change even if Britain left. But a government arguing for an 'In' vote, and its allies in the pro-EU campaign, need to have more to say about the practicalities of what can happen on immigration if Britain does choose to stay in.

Two of the most important policy changes could be at a national, rather than European, level:

(i) Since it cannot promise to directly control the level of EU migration, the government should **make a direct link between the numbers of EU migrants and the resources that go to local areas.**

Higher levels of EU immigration do create pressure on local services, but also means more people in the UK working and paying taxes. It would make a difference if the public could see that those resources didn't disappear into the Treasury coffers, but do follow the flows of people around the country.

When immigration is above the tens of thousands target, that should be seen to trigger an increase in resources to the Government's new Controlling Immigration Fund, with a formula that means those resources are directed to the areas of most rapid change. This policy would require better and faster monitoring of population changes, which is necessary to ensure that if Boston, Grimsby or Southampton are hosting large proportions of EU migrants, people can see how the funding to pay for the school places, doctor's surgeries and housing needs will follow flows of population more quickly than in the past. The government could consult on whether requiring EU migrants to register locally would assist with this – a practice which is mandatory in Germany and the Netherlands.

(ii) **Integration** is the second key area where more practical action is needed to manage immigration better. There is strong agreement that the ability to speak English is important for migrants to fully participate in Britain's economy, society and democracy – and for local people to engage with those coming into their community.

The government should set a civic norm and expectation that everyone in Britain for a year or more should know English, or be learning it. It should engage with employers, councils and educational providers to secure broad commitment to this vision, and to helping overcome the barriers to achieving it. European migrants themselves will often strongly agree with and champion this principle too: it was certainly very strongly held by the Polish participants in our Southampton research, rather to the surprise of their British counterparts.

Free English language lessons at the point of use, with a loan payback scheme to pay tuition costs, as proposed by David Goodhart of Demos,[19] should be implemented to fill provision gaps. More broadly, national and local government should consult employers, particularly in industries and areas that attract a large number of EU migrants such as food processing and hospitality, about what more they could be doing to facilitate and encourage language learning and positive contact between migrants and local communities generally. Different approaches might be relevant and effective in different employment settings, such as agriculture or in retail – but it is reasonable to ask those who see EU migration as important for their businesses to do more to get involved in securing local confidence in how it can work.

Not everybody in the 'Remain' camp will be happy with an approach that, at first glance, appears to concede one of its opponents' key arguments. But the pro-European side can talk more confidently, and to more than two-thirds of the country, if it stops running away from the argument and bases its defence of free movement on a constructive plan to manage migration better, as part of a club that we are in. A referendum means that the public get to decide whether we remain club members, and so continue to play by these rules, with changes that Britain and its fellow members should agree.

MAKING IMMIGRATION WORK IN SOUTHAMPTON

In towns and cities where the pace of change has been rapid, migrants and British-born residents have a shared interest in managing the impacts of immigration to make it work on the ground.

In the course of its research into public attitudes to immigration and the EU, British Future has twice been to Southampton to conduct research groups.

The first time was in 2013, ahead of the lifting of free movement controls on workers from Romania and Bulgaria, when we spoke with long-standing Southampton locals about their views on immigration from Europe, as part of the research for our December 2013 publication "EU migration from Romania and Bulgaria: what does the public think?"

The second was in March 2015, when we brought together British-born Southampton residents and Polish migrants to the city to share their experiences of EU migration. We discussed how to deal with its impacts on issues like public services and benefits, culture and identity, and jobs and the local economy.

We found striking levels of agreement between British and Polish residents about some of the cornerstones of integration that are needed for immigration to work: contribution, both to the community and through paying taxes, and the importance of being able to speak English.

"Some people think they don't need to learn English – that there will be enough Polish people that they can get by. That they can get somebody to translate for them. I think that's too lazy. If you came to this country, then there will be opportunities here that you would not get in Poland. If you don't take those, then you've forgotten why you've come". – Polish migrant to Southampton

"We're in England. We came here. We can't expect to come to England and expect everybody to speak Polish. I explain this to other Polish people too. I say, think about how happy you are, when somebody might find out a single word of Polish, and they say that to you, that's very friendly. Well, how do you think they feel if you come here but don't try to learn any English?". – Polish migrant to Southampton

"I found it really surprising that most of you don't like it if people don't learn English. I had never thought about it. I had never thought that you would think that" – British Southampton resident

ICM polling for British Future's report *EU migration from Romania and Bulgaria: what does the public think?* found that 77% of the public agree "If Romanians and Bulgarians want to stay in Britain they've got to work hard and pay taxes, learn the language, be part of the community. If they do that they'll find we welcome people who make the effort."[20]

Whatever might or might not happen if we leave, there is simply no credible way that levels of net migration could be guaranteed to fall to significantly below 100,000 a year over the next five to ten years while we remain in the EU.

Those whose top political priority is to reduce the numbers of migrants to the lowest level possible would therefore be rational to vote "out" – and most of them will. If people absolutely want to prioritise having the lowest immigration numbers possible, they should leave the EU – and make choices from outside that are compatible with that preference. That would mean rejecting the terms on offer to EFTA members who have free trade agreements with the EU that include free movement as part of the deal. If advocates of Brexit want to argue that Britain would achieve a deal that no other non-EU member has, they may face a high credibility hurdle.

> *"Those whose top political priority is to reduce the numbers of migrants to the lowest level possible would therefore be rational to vote 'Out' – and most of them will."*

Switzerland is outside the European Union, but has been part of EU free trade and free movement. In February 2014, a close vote saw 50.3% support a plan for immigration quotas, instead of the current free movement rules. The government has until 2017 to try to implement this, but has not found a formula to square the circle, since free movement forms part of Switzerland's bilateral deal with the EU. In November 2015, over 100,000 signatures were collected for the "out of a dead end" campaign, seeking to revoke the vote against free movement. The most recent polling shows 61% of Swiss voters support the U-turn, not because free movement is popular, but because most support the idea that the benefits of the bilateral accords make free movement a price worth paying. The Swiss vote will again be sharply contested on both sides – but it certainly shows that leaving the EU is not itself sufficient to impose quotas and controls on EU migration.

At present, it is far from clear that there would be a policy for a post-EU Britain which would be workable, popular and deliver much lower migration levels. Those who want to exit would have the chance to come up with such a plan – but they might need to give people a much clearer idea of what it would be, in order to persuade a majority to take the leap.

Immigration is a big issue in British politics. Being in the EU constrains the policy choices open to governments and public. That is one reason why the referendum is important: it makes very clear that the free movement rules are not a question of having "no choice". We do have the choice to stay in the club or to leave it and the referendum gives us all the responsibility to make that choice. It is a choice that voters will take seriously – and they will want new information from both sides to be able to make it.

We have the choice to leave – and to make alternate arrangements from the outside – though those offering this option may need to tell the voters what the new arrangements might be, if they wish to secure their support.

A majority vote to stay in is an endorsement of free movement, at least as a price which most think is worth paying, if handled better, for the broader benefits of being part of the European club. That would have a profound effect on the immigration debate after the EU referendum.

Once we know the referendum result, there will have to be a new debate about immigration politics and policy before the political parties produce their 2020 election manifestoes. Before we know the result of the EU vote, it is hard to plan ahead, but this will be one of the most significant political challenges facing future contenders to be Prime Minister – firstly, in the Conservative party's choice of David Cameron's successor, and then in the General Election between the parties.

> *"A vote to remain in the EU must, surely, close the phase of the immigration debate in which numbers are trumps."*

If Britain votes to leave, it will open up the question of what choices we make to create a new immigration policy for both EU and non-EU migration. That will have to dig deeper into the trade-offs between the pressures and gains of immigration, if Britain is to have a manageable system of immigration controls that doesn't cut out the gains of immigration such as students, skills and staffing for public services like the NHS. These are not just beneficial to the economy and society; they are broadly popular with the general public too.

If Britain votes to stay, it would surely entrench the existing consensus that the current immigration framework is broken. Indeed, it isn't working for anybody – with growing public frustration about broken promises, along with concerns from the NHS and business about new curbs on skilled workers. A vote to remain in the EU must, surely, close the phase of the immigration debate in which numbers are trumps – because the public would have eschewed the opportunity to put on the agenda at least a possible option for achieving significantly lower numbers. Those seeking to secure public consent for immigration would have to engage the public on the three core issues of public concern – an effective system that works; an approach that ensures and rewards contribution; and the effective promotion of integration – rather than continuing to make promises they can't keep.

Immigration will be important in the referendum campaign, though both sides may decide that they would prefer it wasn't dominant. But it is bound to matter in this campaign – because the choice that the British public makes will shape the immigration policy we have in the decades ahead.

EVENTS, DEAR BOY, EVENTS

The potential impact of unexpected events on the outcome is an important "known unknown" about the referendum. At a time of such international volatility – in economics, security and politics – it would be surprising if there were no surprise events. Our failure to predict the economic crash of 2008 or many of the political twists and turns of recent years have led to a significant slump in sales of crystal balls.

For events to become potential referendum 'game-changers', they need to have an extremely high level of public salience, dominating the British front-pages and our public conversation with a sustained profile at a crucial time when many are making their minds up. Many events of significant geopolitical importance may often not meet that threshold.

The crisis of the Euro and Greece's dramatic stand-off, for example, did dominate the news for a fortnight; but while the ongoing debate over the future of the Eurozone will surely have important economic and political impacts, it is followed predominantly by a smaller, more highly engaged audience. The conflict involving Russia in Ukraine even redrew the map of the continent – but many Britons will not recall much about it, beyond a vague impression of President Putin earning the ire of European leaders.

The Syrian refugee crisis had affected millions over the last four years. While many people have lost their lives making the treacherous journey across the Mediterranean, it was only in September 2015 that it was catapulted to a new degree of prominence, both by the scale of refugee flows and the public response to the picture of the drowned body of three-year-old Aylan Kurdi.

The refugee crisis is likely to affect how people think about the referendum choice because it is a highly salient event that dramatises one of the key themes of the referendum: immigration. However, the public response to events may often be polarised – certainly between those who are strongly anti- and strongly pro-EU – and give both sides the familiar challenge of reaching the centre. Whenever any advocate believes that they can seize on the breakthrough issue that will decide the referendum, it is always worth checking if that is an argument likely to mobilise their existing support, or to reach the 'anxious middle'.

The public reaction to the refugee crisis did not significantly shift public attitudes overall, but it did polarise them on both sides of the debate. Ipsos MORI research[21] has shown that 23% of people took some form of action – signing petitions or donating money or clothes – in favour of refugees in the Autumn. Between a quarter and a third of people wanted Britain to take more refugees, with around a quarter of people believing that Angela Merkel's response was much better than David Cameron's, and that Britain should take part in EU refugee quotas, something backed by 25% and opposed by 65%. It is unsurprising that those who take that view are overwhelmingly committed supporters of EU membership. At the same time, polls have shown just under 30% of people believing Britain should take no refugees at all – consistent with the general 'shut the border' views on all forms of migration of around one in four people. Again, it should be no surprise to find that those holding that opinion are very determined that we should leave the EU.

The anxious middle – more likely to be referendum swing voters – were conflicted, feeling the pull of both sides of the argument. They wanted Britain to respond to the crisis and to take some refugees from Syria; but they were cautious about how many we could take, given high levels of immigration and potential pressures on housing. The response of the government – with David Cameron taking 20,000 refugees over four years – was pretty close to the views of this 'conflicted middle' majority.

Public concern about immigration rose in response to the crisis. The issue returned, ahead of the economy and the NHS, as the number one issue of concern, with 55% seeing it as an important issue.[22] This is often reported simply as an increase in immigration scepticism, implying that everybody who is concerned is anti-migration. That is partly true, but the details show that the increase in salience reflects both broad public scepticism and some increase in empathy for refugees too. Of the 55% who said immigration was a top issue, half (49%) said this was because 'there are too many immigrants coming – we need to reduce numbers' – while one in five (19%) of said that it should be a priority issue because "I'm worried about refugees – and want Britain to do more to help".

Overall, these findings mean that a quarter of the whole population are 'high concern' migration sceptics, while a tenth are 'high concern' pro-migration liberals. These groups are much more likely to be committed to one side or another of the referendum debate than to be undecided. Intriguingly over a quarter (27%) of those who see immigration as a top issue said "both" – believing Britain should do more for refugees, while reducing immigration overall. That means that nearly half of those with high immigration concerns were expressing empathy for refugees.

Both sides of the referendum debate will certainly want to make a case about how and why our EU membership either makes cooperation on these challenges more effective, for 'Remain', or constrains our choices and creates additional risk, for 'Leave'.

Because high public concern about illegal immigration is dramatised by images from Calais, many people also naturally connect that to the question of Britain's relationship with the European Union. It is difficult to see, however, why somebody trying to cross the border in the back of a lorry would change their mind if Britain's EU membership status were different. The 'Remain' camp argue that this issue would become more difficult – because leaving the EU would put in question the ability to police the British border in Calais, not Dover; while the 'Leave' campaign suggest new bilateral arrangements with France could still be possible.

The European Union has introduced a programme to share a limited number of refugees around the EU. This has been highly contentious, particularly in central and Eastern Europe. Britain is not part of the scheme and there is very limited public appetite in the UK for us to participate in such a quota programme. The British debate has been about a national decision to protect refugees – with the UK government wanting to say to its EU partners that the country is 'doing its bit' both in resettling refugees from UN camps, and in providing the largest amount of aid to the region.

Security concerns, particularly following the terrorist attack on Paris, could well lead to significant reforms of the visa-free Schengen zone – involving 22 countries – but Britain has never been part of the Schengen agreement (which, somewhat counterintuitively, does cover four countries that are not in the EU, including Switzerland and Norway).

For 'Remain' the key risk is less at the level of policy, more the corrosive impact if there is a broad perception that the EU cannot cope with the challenges that it faces. When voters see televised images of Greece's overflowing refugee reception centres, movements of people across the continent with states closing borders or passing on their responsibilities to others, and then worry about whether someone might climb into their car boot when they return from holiday on the Calais ferry, it does not give the impression that the system of European cooperation is working well. This is only compounded by the instincts of refugee protection advocates to emphasise the enormous human scale of the refugee crisis. A pragmatic focus, on actions that show that the crisis is manageable, may be more effective.

For 'Leave', it might mean some caution about the idea of winning the referendum on an anti-refugee and pro-security platform. UKIP leader Nigel Farage was quick to respond to the Paris murders by attacking free movement – "This dream of the free movement of people, this dream for others of the Schengen area. It hasn't just meant the free movement of people, it has meant the free movement of Kalashnikov rifles. It has meant the free movement of terrorists, and it has meant the free movement of jihadists."[23]

That will have resonated strongly with UKIP's strongest supporters. The broader public will certainly want our government to keep British citizens safe – but may be sceptical of letting an ISIS attack on civilians dictate that we back down on our commitment to protect some of the world's most vulnerable people. Revulsion at ISIS will certainly resonate strongly across Britain – but people know this threat will exist in and out of the EU. A 'Leave' campaign which puts the jihadi threat front and centre will resonate strongly with its base; but that tone and approach might well be questioned by many others whom the Brexit campaign would need to persuade.

6. *IN IT FOR THE MONEY?*
HOW TO TALK ABOUT EUROPE AND
THE ECONOMY

"Would we better off in or out?" If voters could ask one question before they decide, that would be the one that many people would choose. But if undecided voters are hoping that somebody will simply set out 'the answer' to that question, in a straightforward, unbiased and uncontested way, then they are bound to be frustrated and disappointed by the referendum campaign to come.

Voters will hear campaigners state that EU membership costs every person £900 a year – or makes everybody £3000 a year better off. They will be told that being in the EU adds up to 5 per cent to our GDP, and that it reduces it by 10 per cent or more, depending on which study you want to look at.

The economic impacts of Britain being in or out will certainly be one of the central arguments of the referendum. So we are all going to have to find a way to navigate our way through a blizzard of claims and counter-claims about every aspect of Britain's relationship with the European Union, and the potential upsides and downsides of our future inside or outside the club.

Both of the campaigns will face significant challenges about how to cut through the noise to make their case beyond their existing supporters. The referendum debate also presents significant challenges for other voices who could help to inform the public's choice. Yet they may look at the heated debate and polarised politics of a hard-fought referendum and decide that it is better to stay out of the kitchen, choosing *not* to talk about Europe, rather than making their contribution to inform the public's decision.

WHY 'THE REAL FACTS' CAN'T LAND A KNOCKOUT BLOW IN THE REFERENDUM

'I wish somebody would just give me the facts' is a natural plea from the undecided voter – especially if they feel that they have limited time to follow every twist and turn of the referendum arguments, but want to take seriously this choice for Britain, its economy and the future opportunities of young people.

Referendums are never going to work out like that. Naturally, both sides are going to build up and persuade for their case – and seek to knock the rival case. This will mobilise and enthuse supporters of both sides, who will be excited to see their side finally 'get the real facts across' and 'bust the myths' and misunderstandings pushed by their opponents.

"Both sides fire a lot of facts and figures at you, which they bandy around. Facts and figures – in the end, you believe what you want to believe. They are both as convincing as each other. That's the problem. And you don't know – well I can't quite make my mind up – which side is being honest with the figures," said one voter, part of a group of undecided voters asked by the BBC 10 o'clock news to watch the televised debate on EU membership between Nick Clegg and Nigel Farage in the Spring of 2014.

That offers a pre-echo of how the referendum argy-bargy may look to those who haven't decided. It is an experience which will be exacerbated by the broadcasting rules which, to ensure fair and balanced coverage, will be legally compelled to give equal airtime to both sides over contested referendum questions. If a political or business voice says that Britain will be better off in, they will invariably be followed by an alternative voice saying the opposite. Unless you have a strong pre-disposition to trust one messenger over the other, most viewers and listeners will again be left mainly with the impression that the issue under discussion is the subject of disagreement.

THE FACTS STILL MATTER ... BUT IT'S A QUESTION OF JUDGEMENTS ABOUT UNCERTAINTY TOO ...

Even if facts do rather less to persuade citizens than many people think, it would still be unsatisfactory to take an 'anything goes' approach that gives up entirely on the idea of seeking to have a well-informed public debate about such an important choice. So it will be useful for there to be rigorous attempts from expert voices to keep both sides honest, through media fact-checking and experts trying to verify the statements of the campaigners on both sides. The way that the Institute of Fiscal Studies scrutinizes tax and spending plans in general elections, for example, plays an important role in helping to provide more informed media coverage – but parties and candidates will rarely ditch arguments that have been challenged, instead saying that they don't accept the assumptions of the model.

Nevertheless, this kind of scrutiny could enable voters – at least those motivated to pay enough attention to the TV and radio coverage – to start to get a clearer sense of what is known about the benefits and costs of Britain's current EU membership, and the shape of the argument about what we put in and what we get out.

It will be considerably harder, however, to paint an accurate factual picture of the competing arguments about alternative future options, which inevitably involve more speculative hypotheses about what might happen. So arguments about facts will be part of this referendum – but this is bound to end up being a question of judgements about uncertainties too.

"Arguments about facts will be part of this referendum – but this is bound to end up being a question of judgements about uncertainties too."

The crisis of the Euro has undoubtedly damaged the European Union's reputation as a driver of prosperity. The Eurozone recovery has underperformed against the UK and other major economies: the overall level of economic activity remains behind the pre-crash levels of eight years ago, while UK GDP went past its 2007 peak in 2014.

While the Euro was a political as well as an economic project for those who joined it, its design flaws partly reflected the lack of political appetite among Euro members for the level of economic policy coordination that a shared currency requires.[24] Major clashes, particularly between Germany and other member states, have exemplified the difficulties of creating an approach suitable across northern and southern European economies facing distinct economic challenges. Governments of Eurozone countries remain committed to making the Euro work – and there is a broad consensus that the Eurozone will now need some greater degree of economic and political integration among its members.

The nine EU members which are not in the Euro will want a stronger economic recovery among their trading partners, but will need to ensure too that their interests are protected within the wider EU of 28 nations. The British government is making this a core priority of the renegotiation effort, but it seems very likely that the future architecture of the EU and the Eurozone will remain a work in progress when the British voters go to the polls.

British voters could hardly be any more certain that the UK was right to remain outside the Euro. A pan-European Gallup International poll found British voters overwhelmingly opposed to joining the Euro, by 85% to 6%, while opinion across the 13 countries surveyed was evenly split overall, with 44% preferring a national currency and 42% the Euro. It found majorities in favour of the Euro in several countries including Belgium, Ireland and Spain, while a plurality of the public would have preferred to have kept their national currencies in both France and Germany.[25] An important consequence for the British Europe debate is that there is no longer any viable mainstream proposition for Britain to be 'at the heart of Europe', certainly in terms of joining the Eurozone core as those 19 countries embark on a further round of integration. That marks an historic shift in traditional pro-European advocacy.

So the Euro will be a favourite theme of the 'Leave' campaign, not the 'Remain' campaign, during this referendum. Those promoting Brexit will question the credibility of those pro-Europeans who argued, a decade ago, that British influence depended on joining the Euro. If a handful of the most prominent pro-European voices – including Richard Branson, Michael Heseltine and Peter Mandelson – continue to suggest that they have not yet given up on the idea of Britain one day joining the Euro, that will certainly be a welcome gift to those campaigning to leave, allowing Brexit campaigners to try to argue that 'there is no status quo in this referendum', seeking to balance the risks of leaving with potential future risks of staying in a shifting EU.

It is no coincidence that the 'Remain' campaign have chosen a figurehead in businessman Stuart Rose who was always opposed to the Euro – and will now need to make a virtue of Britain's semi-detached status. The Prime Minister has argued that he is seeking a new 'British model' reflecting a 'best of both worlds' approach. The case for 'Remain' may turn out to be that joining the Euro core would be too hot for Britain, but leaving the club entirely would risk going too far into the cold outside. Should that case become countered by a post-Brexit plan to seek to safeguard the economic benefits of membership by negotiating a free trade deal, then the boundaries may begin to blur around what Britain being 'in' or 'out' of a changing EU might mean.

IS THIS VOTE ANY BUSINESS OF BUSINESS?

The undecided referendum voters will listen to the politicians, on both sides, and to the official campaigns. But "they would say that, wouldn't they?" may often be the reaction to their contradictory claims. If the public are seeking a less partisan source on the pros and cons for the economy, many might look to business voices to inform their choice.

Our research finds that business voices are trusted in the EU referendum debate, particularly those from smaller companies who may be able to speak from a more local perspective.

Figure 9: Trust in business voices in the EU referendum debate

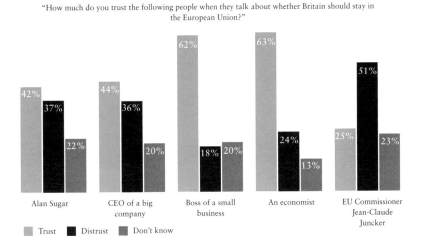

"How much do you trust the following people when they talk about whether Britain should stay in the European Union?"

Some business voices will actively join the campaigns, on one side or the other. A significant number, however, might choose not to talk about Europe, rather than seeking to play any role in informing the public choice.

One survey of businesses this summer, conducted by the Institute of Chartered Secretaries and Administrators and reported in the

Financial Times,[26] found that two-thirds of businesses believed their interests would be adversely affected by a British exit from the European Union, while only 7% planned to speak publicly about this in the referendum.

The instinct to steer clear of the debate is not hard to understand. The EU referendum is bound to be an emotional, partisan and polarised campaign at times. No contribution to it can keep everybody happy. If a close vote looks like splitting the country down the middle, then any large business is likely to find that they will have some employees and customers with strong views on both sides of the debate. It will be tempting to stay out – on the grounds that the business of business is business, not politics.

The point that business should keep quiet might be made in a somewhat more menacing way too. The leading Eurosceptic MP John Redwood made a point of saying that there would be destabilising consequences for businesses who spoke up for British membership of the EU. Redwood said that "those of us organising the 'get out' campaign will then make life difficult for them by making sure that their customers, their employees and their shareholders who disagree with them – and there will be a lot who disagree with them – will be expressing their views very forcefully and will be destabilising their corporate governance".[27]

The Redwood view does sound rather over the top – and it could well appear hypocritical for 'Leave' campaigners to adopt this view, given that much Eurosceptic energy has gone precisely into organising business advocacy, with the Business for Britain campaign for EU reform, doubtless in the hope that many of those involved will support the call to leave as well. However, the threat of disruption may give some boardrooms pause.

The argument for ducking the referendum debate is strengthened in current boardroom conversations by unhappy memories and bruises from Scotland's hard fought referendum in the autumn of 2014. Many businesses did have a strong view about the economic uncertainties of independence, with many crossing their fingers for a vote for Scotland to remain in the UK. Yet most hoped to keep their heads below the parapet during the campaign – not only to avoid alienating customers and employees on either side, but because maintaining good relations with both the Scottish and Westminster governments could be harder if they spoke out. So business voices mostly kept quiet, hoping that there was a plan to deliver the outcome that they hoped for, until ever tightening polls saw a last minute clamour to get involved. It isn't clear how much difference the panicky reaction had on the decision of the Scottish voters, but it caused exactly the public pain that business had sought to avoid.

> *"The referendum would be diminished by the absence of business voices."*

That also raises the question of whether business voices would do any good for their own side anyway. Certainly, neither *Bankers for Brussels* nor *Hedge Funds for Brexit* sound like the most popular of public persuaders.

Yet the referendum would be diminished by the absence of business voices. It would deprive the public of a perspective that they would want to hear from – on some issues of the referendum at least, if not others.

In any event, keeping out entirely will prove a forlorn hope, since businesses will have a duty to prepare for the potential impacts of various referendum outcomes – and to advise shareholders, employees and other stakeholders of their view of the business impacts and risks of different scenarios where relevant. If they may well get dragged in anyway, it would make sense for business leaders to understand what their audiences want to know, what business can sensibly say, and how to communicate effectively with public audiences. The lessons of Scotland counsel against rushing in to the debate at the last minute in response to sudden changes in the final weeks: a more considered approach is needed. One challenge for business, therefore, is to establish what the right terms of engagement might be and what they first need to know in order to do that. So how should business voices prepare to talk about Europe?

First, find out what the voters want to know about from business. Crucially, business leaders need to find out what undecided voters want to know from business in order to inform their choice – and to speak to their specific locus of expertise.

Business does have a proper role in public affairs, as a trusted voice on issues of jobs, growth and investment. Business leaders should find out what voters care about on these topics and what information they expect from business. They should not allow their voice to be silenced by threats from either side. Instead, they can defend their right, and obligation, to speak, often by sticking to the topics on which they can claim expertise and on which voters might look to them for an answer.

"It would help to be clear that they can't and won't presume to tell voters how to vote – and that there will be business voices on both sides of the debate"

It is the legitimacy of the business voice with the undecided, anxious middle, not the passionate antis nor the pro-Europeans, which could guide business's engagement on the issues. These are not ideological voters: the practical consequences of their vote will determine their decision. They are less likely to trust the campaigners and they will be looking for accurate and neutral information from sources they can trust. This is where business will need to play its part. To do so effectively, it will need to establish how to reach the intended audience and present them with information that is helpful, understanding the scope and limits of the role that voters expect it to play.

Secondly, speak to the public interest, not just the business interest.
It would diminish the public debate if business voices could not provide their perspective – whether pro, anti or on the fence. But these voices will have limited reach if they can't link the interests and perspectives of business to what is good for the economy and society generally. Employees, customers and suppliers, and the general public, may want to know about the impact on the local and regional economy as well as on future prospects for employment or trade.

Thirdly, help to identify the questions that need to be answered about what 'In' or 'Out' will mean.
Business voices can help to inform the choice that people make – by providing information about the potential gains and risks of EU membership and the alternatives. The rival campaigns may not want to acknowledge that this is a choice about complexity and uncertainty on both sides. So business voices may be better placed to help deepen the referendum debate, by pushing the rival campaigns to answer some of the difficult questions about the choices and trade-offs involved in debates about the EU and Britain's place within it, or the alternatives after we leave.

Finally, inform people's choice – don't threaten or tell them what to decide.
The months ahead of the referendum campaign itself offer an opportunity for business leaders to find out what voters want to understand about the impact on business and the economy of

membership of the European Union, so as to help people make a well-informed decision.

It would help to be clear that they can't and won't presume to tell voters how to vote – and that there will be business voices on both sides of the debate.

Business voices should recognize the limits as well as the scope of their voice. The referendum won't only be about the economy: it will also about identity, democracy and sovereignty – and many other issues on which business can claim no special locus or expertise. But the impact of this choice on Britain's economy *is* the business of business – and so business leaders can and should bring their distinctive expertise to bear in this debate.

ON THE MONEY: THE CHALLENGE FOR THE 'REMAIN' AND 'LEAVE' CAMPAIGNS

Both sides are going to find it difficult to break through – to their increasing frustration, given their shared, albeit opposing convictions that they are evidently in the right.

Many 'In' advocates are convinced that theirs is the side of reason against emotion. They see their problem to be one of getting 'the real facts' to be heard over the more emotional, populist and media-friendly arguments of those who want to leave the EU; and of making people finally see that the balance of evidence makes it clear that there is only one sensible choice. Unsurprisingly, 'Out' advocates take a rather different view of the role of evidence in the EU debate. They see the 'In' side as offering a complacent, fixed, Establishment view which would be 'In' regardless of the evidence, and which has therefore failed to change its arguments even as Europe's economic prospects have faltered in the era of the Euro. The problem, as they see it, is getting people to wake-up and see that this Europhile emperor has no clothes – and that Britain should not see any risk in departure.

Each of these is largely a comfort zone explanation. Pro-EU advocates who think the role is to 'get the evidence across' appear oblivious to a growing body of evidence in political psychology that facts are rarely as influential as they would like to think. The 'Leave' campaign will need to ensure that its conviction that the opponents' arguments don't stack up doesn't simply descend into a form of 'say it louder' Euroscepticism – one which has much to say about what's wrong with the status quo but has fewer answers to the practical questions about what happens next.

Of course, neither side can afford to depart the field of battle, so much energy will be spent on claim and counter-claim, rebuttal and pre-buttal.

Arguably, that presents a bigger campaign challenge for the 'Remain' than the 'Leave' campaign, even though the economy is considered 'home' territory for them, and certainly rather more comfortable ground than trying to work out what to say about immigration or identity. As our ICM polling shows, the economy is the top reason for choosing 'In' and the main doubt many people have about choosing to leave the EU. However, what that also means is that the 'In' side does need to *win* the economic argument in the referendum campaign. The 'In' campaign would be unwise to try to make people love Europe, still less the EU institutions in Brussels. But they do need to persuade people that there is some significant economic benefit to being in the EU, in order to make the frustrations of having to negotiate with 27 other countries, and the limits of being bound by agreed rules, a price worth paying for club membership.

The 'Leave' campaign, arguably, will have done enough if it could neutralise the economy as a referendum theme. So a polarised debate which demonstrates that there are two sides of the story – and a counter-argument for every argument – could be enough to do that, if people have another reason to want to get out, such as immigration or sovereignty. Strategists on both sides have identified a key group of 'head over heart' voters: as 'Leave' strategist Dominic Cummings put it, "A fifth that would like to leave but are worried about the impact on living standards."[28]

The biggest challenge for 'Leave', however, is that the uncertainty of a hotly contested campaign could also leave voters with a clear sense that their questions, about what would happen next, have not all been answered. It will be very difficult for 'Leave' to convincingly answer the "What does 'out' look like?" question, given that it depends on a negotiation with EU members that would not take place until after the vote; but many undecided or wavering voters will be reluctant to lend them their votes until they do so.

7. *MAKING OUR MINDS UP –* HOW TO HAVE A REFERENDUM THAT'S GOOD FOR BRITAIN

The referendum is a big choice for a Britain. It's also a binary one – there's no middle option. So it will be divisive. We should, however, do all we can to ensure that the only divisions are over whether people think Britain should be in the EU or not. We don't do culture wars in this country and we don't need them.

This isn't a fight between young and old, north and south, university educated or not, migrant and native. It's a debate between all Britons about the future of the country we all share. If its done right, it could reveal a lot more common ground between 'In' and 'Out' than most people think. So we want a fair fight and a referendum that's good for Britain. And that means three things.

> *"If its done right, it will reveal a lot more common ground between 'In' and 'Out' than most people think."*

Firstly, participation: the referendum is big decision for the country and its people – and as many of them as possible should be involved in deciding it. This is a choice that affects all of us, not just the people who care most about it. That's a big challenge: most people don't really understand or care very much about Europe. They don't see how it affects them, or what difference choosing 'Leave' or 'Remain' will make to their lives. Both sides of the debate should rise to this challenge – and agree that a big referendum is a good referendum.

Second, those who take part in this big decision should have a very clear sense of what it is they're deciding. Both 'In' and 'Out' should give voters a clear sense of what it means to put their cross in their respective boxes on the ballot paper. If there is going to be a significant shift in the relationship between Britain and countries in the Eurozone, voters should know what that means before they vote and not one or two years later. 'Out' need also to be as clear as possible about what the set-up will look like outside the EU – if we can only get a free trade deal by agreeing to free movement too, the electorate should know about it.

This is a challenge for Prime Minister David Cameron too. His renegotiation of Britain's relationship with the EU has been shrouded in secrecy, or at least obscurity. The electorate has a right to know the details of whatever 'deal' the PM comes back with from Brussels. There should be no surprises a few years down the line.

Thirdly this should be, as far as is possible, a definitive decision on Britain's relationship with Europe. One side or other is certain to be unhappy with the result – but they will have to suck it up and accept it. Referendums are expensive and they consume political energy which could be expended elsewhere. While the losers, whether they be Europhiles or Eurosceptics, will be spoiling for another fight as soon as their cuts and bruises have healed, most of the public won't.

Of course there could be extenuating circumstances – if there are huge changes to the political or economic circumstances of Britain or our European neighbours a few years later, a plausible case might be made for putting the question once again. But there will be no public appetite for a 'Neverendum' once people have answered the question once. This is your chance and you've got to take it.

A referendum in which most people participate, where they feel they've been given a clear and fair choice, will help ensure that the decision we make has democratic legitimacy. So we should start there.

Getting this right will help ensure we get a fair, legitimate and definitive decision. It may also help to revitalise our democracy. Scotland's referendum on independence may have polarised opinions and it may at times have got overheated – but it also left a legacy of increased engagement in politics.

We could do with some of that right across the country – taking political debate out of the Westminster bubble and engaging the public in the decisions that will affect them and their families. If we achieve that, then whatever the result this referendum could be good for Britain.

THE CASE FOR A 'THIRD CAMPAIGN' TO INCREASE PARTICIPATION

Britain has seen one of the best and one of the worst recent examples of how a referendum can succeed, or fail, in engaging citizens. Scotland's independence referendum did not just see an 85% turnout; it has created a legacy of greater political engagement and interest in Scotland. By contrast, most people will have long forgotten that they were given the chance to decide on whether to change Britain's electoral system in May 2011, with just 42% of people taking part, even when local elections were being held on the same day.

Whatever the outcome of the EU referendum, it would be good for political engagement to have the maximum possible participation in the vote.

A nationwide 'Third Campaign' should be launched – with the simple goal of maximising participation in the referendum, and finding effective ways to spread the message that Britain has a big decision to make and that everybody should be part of it.

The independence, integrity and neutrality of such a campaign should be paramount. The Electoral Commission should oversee a process by which the most effective plans to increase registration and turnout are assessed by independent experts – with the best campaign ideas given some public funding. It would also provide an effective focal point to attract pro bono support from the great and good of advertising and PR, as well as an important source of advice to employers, charities and to the national and local media, about how they can support the effort to get everybody involved in making Britain's big decision.

The Third Campaign should be allocated free-to-air broadcasting during the campaign period, like the official 'Remain' and 'Leave' campaigns' own referendum broadcasts. To help protect the neutrality of the Third Campaign, the 'Remain' and 'Leave' campaigns should be invited to play a role – by nominating individuals who can provide constructive oversight to maintain confidence that it sticks to the cause of maximising turnout in ways that are neutral and fair to both campaigns.

The Third Campaign should also produce guidance for schools and colleges, businesses, charities and other employers, on effective ways to encourage people to participate, while remaining neutral on the referendum question. Some organisations will also want to take sides in the referendum, which is perfectly legitimate for those that make that choice. But there is also a crucial role for advice for those who do not wish to take sides. Given the heat of a referendum campaign, that will be vital to ensure that organisations do not shy away from playing this constructive civic role in the public interest for fear that such benign activity might be risky or controversial.

We reject the view that maximum participation would axiomatically favour one side or the other in the referendum. The truth is that we simply don't know how people who have not heard the arguments will respond when they do hear them for the first time. The 16–18 year olds given the vote in Scotland did not vote as many had predicted they might. Rather, the decision to enfranchise them saw a great many attend and take part in school debates and pay attention to the media, before making their own minds up for themselves.

Kenny Imafidon of political engagement campaigners Bite the Ballot, who are backing our call for a Third Campaign, said:

"It is essential we inspire voters to get engaged in political discussions about the pros and cons of Europe, replicating the success of Scotland's referendum which breathed new life into its politics.

"Both campaigns must ensure that participation is their first priority and second, that they present facts and avoid sensationalised stories that prevent people from making informed decisions.

"This is a massive decision for all citizens here in the UK and one that we should not leave to others to make for us! Everyone must have a say."

There are low turnout segments of society who, at the outset, appear to lean both in and out – young voters are thought to be more pro-European, while 'DE' unskilled workers are usually more Eurosceptic. A Third Campaign could usefully seek specific civic partners to help engage with young voters, with unskilled workers, with rural voters, with ethnic minorities, and with women who didn't go to university – as some of the groups likely to need more encouragement to take part.

So both campaigns could play an important role by supporting calls for a high turnout. They should commit to taking this historic opportunity to make their case to those who have not heard the arguments before. That would be a much better response to this democratic challenge than somehow seeking to 'game' the referendum by simply trying to mobilise their own vocal minorities more effectively than their rivals.

Whichever side of the argument they are on, the case for taking the debate to as many people as possible is one thing upon which everybody should be able to agree.

8. NOTES AND TABLES

NOTES

1. For pan-EU analysis of mildly greater Euroscepticism, see Brent F.Nelsen and James L.Guth:
    Exploring the Gender Gap: *Women, Men and Public Attitudes toward European Integration*
    (European Union Politics) October 2000
    British Election Study 2014–17 internet panel, cited in Goodwin and Milazzo: *UKIP: Inside
    the campaign to redraw the map of British politics* (2015) page 310 shows 47% of Remain
    voters and 50% of Leave voters were women in the May 2015 wave; while two-thirds of
    don't knows were women. Also see Eurobarometer http://ec.europa.eu/public_opinion/
    index_en.htm

2. Prof John Curtice, *So who voted yes and who voted no? What Scotland Thinks, September 2014*
    http://blog.whatscotlandthinks.org/2014/09/voted-yes-voted/

3. Omar Khan and Debbie Weekes-Bernard, *This is still about us. Why ethnic minorities think
    differently about immigration, Runnymede Trust, December 2015* http://www.runnymedetrust.org/

4. *How to talk about immigration,* British Future 2014 http://www.britishfuture.org/wp-content/
    uploads/2014/11/How-To-Talk-About-Immigration-FINAL.pdf

5. Drew Weston, *'The political brain: the role of emotion in deciding the fate of the nation'*
    (Public Affairs, 2008) and www.politicalbrain.com

6. The Times, 23 November, *'How Farage went to war with UKIP's only MP'* http://www.thetimes.
    co.uk/tto/news/politics/article4620910.ece

7. *This way to Brexit: what would happen if Britain left the EU?* John Harris, The Guardian
    10 October 2014 http://www.theguardian.com/politics/2014/oct/10/this-way-to-brexit-what-
    would-happen-if-britain-left-eu

8. President Charles de Gaulle, press conference, 14 January 1963 http://toryreformgroup.
    tumblr.com/post/56968234215/de-gaulle-was-right-to-veto-britains-eec

9. Hugo Young, *This Blessed Plot – Britain and Europe from Churchill to Blair,* Macmillian 1999

10. Daniel Hannan MEP, 1 December 2009, on the Lisbon treaty taking legal effect.

11. YouGov for The Times October 2014 https://d25d2506sfb94s.cloudfront.net/cumulus_
    uploads/document/leic6gw6vq/TimesResults_141028_ChangingBritain_W.pdf

12. Douglas Carswell speaking at a British Future event at the Palace of Westminster,
    24 February 2015 http://www.britishfuture.org/articles/news/douglas-carswell-mp-positive-
    immigration/

13. *The politics of immigration,* British Future May 2015 http://www.britishfuture.org/wp-content/uploads/2015/09/The-politics-of-immigration.pdf

14. Douglas Carswell speaking at a British Future event at the Palace of Westminster, 24 February 2015 http://www.britishfuture.org/articles/news/douglas-carswell-mp-positive-immigration/

15. Nigel Farage speaking to the Daily Express, September 2015 http://www.express.co.uk/news/politics/603638/Seize-moment-Nigel-Farage-rallies-Britons-vote-NO-EU-referendum

16. Dominic Cummings, *'My report for Business for Britain on the dynamics of the debate over the EU, and a small but telling process point on the EU'*, June 2014. https://dominiccummings.wordpress.com/2014/06/30/my-report-for-business-for-britain-on-the-dynamics-of-the-debate-over-the-eu-and-a-small-but-telling-process-point-on-the-eu/

17. ONS migration quarterly report, November 2015 http://www.ons.gov.uk/ons/rel/migration1/migration-statistics-quarterly-report/november-2015/index.html

18. NatCen's British Social Attitudes 31 http://www.bsa.natcen.ac.uk/latest-report/british-social-attitudes-31/immigration/introduction.aspx

19. David Goodhart of Demos, Proposed in his book *'The British Dream'* http://www.amazon.co.uk/The-British-Dream-Successes-Immigration/dp/1843548054

20. *EU migration from Romania and Bulgaria: what does the public think?* British Future, http://www.britishfuture.org/publication/eu-migration-from-romania-and-bulgaria-what-does-the-public-think/

21. Ipsos MORI interviewed a representative sample of 1,941 British online adults aged 16+ years between 15–19 October. Interviews were conducted on Ipsos' online panel and results have been weighted by demographic factors to represent the British population.

22. Economist/Ipsos MORI *October 2015 Issues Index* https://www.ipsos-mori.com/researchpublications/researcharchive/3646/Level-of-concern-about-housing-is-highest-in-40-years-though-immigration-still-dominates.aspx

23. Nigel Farage speech in Basingstoke 16 November 2015 http://www.independent.co.uk/news/uk/politics/nigel-farage-says-the-eu-has-allowed-the-free-movement-of-kalashnivov-rifles-and-jihadists-a6737501.html

24. *European attitudes towards the EU: Britain sticks out, ORB International,* http://www.opinion.co.uk/article.php?s=european-attitudes-towards-the-eu-britain-stands-out

25. http://www.opinion.co.uk/perch/resources/global-we-tables-weight1-v6.pdf

26. *UK companies fear speaking out on Brexit,* Financial Times 12 July 2015 http://www.ft.com/cms/s/0/9bb67f78-23f6-11e5-bd83-71cb60e8f08c.html#axzz3tHRUfKAP

27. *Tory John Redwood warns businesses not to stand in way of EU exit,* The Guardian, 29 September 2014 http://www.theguardian.com/world/2014/sep/29/john-redwood-warns-businesses-stand-way-eu-exit

28. *Vote Leave's Monthly Big Picture Update.* Oct 30 2015 http://www.voteleavetakecontrol.org/151030_campaign_news

DATA TABLES

This pamphlet features original analysis drawing on attitudinal research by ICM for British Future conducted 19–21 August 2015 and research by Survation for British Future conducted immediately after the General Election from 8–15 May 2015, as well as polling already in the public domain.

Figure 1: Thinking about a possible referendum on Britain's EU membership, which of the following best sums up your current voting intention?

	Number of People
Leaning Out	25
Out	19
Leaning In	25
In	17
Don't know	14

ICM for British Future, August 2015

Figure 2: Why do people want to stay in or get out of the EU?

	Economy	Ease of Travel	Change is too risky
In	57	12	11

	Decisions affecting Britain should be made only in Britain	Immigration	Economy
Out	47	32	9

ICM for British Future, August 2015

Figure 3: The 'don't know' referendum gender gap

	Men	Women
May (YouGov)	13	21
May/June (ICM)	14	26
June (YouGov)	13	25
June (YouGov)	11	24
July (YouGov)	14	22
Aug (Survation)	15	25
Aug (YouGov)	12	20
Sept (Survation)	16	24
Sept (ICM)	12	22
Oct (ICM)	11	22
Oct (ICM)	13	23
Oct (ICM)	12	22
Oct/Nov (ICM)	13	22

YouGov (May, June, July, August 2015), Survation (August, September 2015) and ICM, (May, June, September, October, November 2015)

Figure 4: How much do you trust the following people when they talk about whether Britain should remain in the EU?

	Trust	Distrust	Don't know
Tony Blair	28	59	13
Nigel Farage	36	54	11
Nick Clegg	39	48	13
David Cameron	49	41	10

Survation for British Future, May 2015

Figure 5: What does the public think of the people running the in and out campaigns?

	In	Out
Positive agenda	20	13
Negative agenda	9	26
In touch with the concerns of ordinary people	12	25
Out of touch with the concerns of ordinary people	24	14

ICM for British Future, August 2015

Figure 6: How do you describe your national identity?

	England	Scotland
British	47	23
English	40	
Scottish		65
European	4	2

NatCen's British Social Attitudes 2014

Figures for those who only gave one answer when asked to describe their national identity, and answers to follow-up question 'And if you had to choose, which one terms best describes the way you think of yourself?

Figure 7: How EU referendum voting intention corresponds with views on immigration

	Migration Liberals	Anxious Middle	Migration sceptics
Out	10	15	43
Leaning Out	17	29	30
Leaning In	28	30	12
In	37	14	2
Don't know	8	12	13

ICM for British Future, August 2015

Figure 8: Ipsos MORI Issues Index – Immigration vs EU – last 25 years

Source: www.ipsos-mori.com

Figure 9: How much do you trust the following people when they talk about whether Britain should stay in the European Union?

	Trust	Distrust	Don't know
Sir Alan Sugar	42	37	22
CEO of a big company	44	36	20
Boss of a small business	62	18	20
An economist	63	24	13
EU Commissioner Jean Claude Juncker	25	51	23

Survation for British Future, May 2015

9. ABOUT BRITISH FUTURE

British Future is an independent, non-partisan thinktank engaging people's hopes and fears about integration and migration, opportunity and identity, so that we share a confident and welcoming Britain, inclusive and fair to all.

Since British Future's founding in 2012 we have conducted research on public attitudes to these issues in the UK, projecting our findings publicly to inform national debate.

Our attitudinal research has contributed to national discussions on issues including how attitudes to immigration affected the 2015 General Election; ethnic minority voting behaviour; immigration from the European Union; attitudes to international students in the UK; Englishness and what it means to the English; the hopes and fears of first-time voters; and racism, discrimination and national identity in modern Britain.

Other publications from British Future can be found online:

The Politics of Immigration – the surprising lessons of the 2015 General Election and what they mean for party leaders, **May 2015** draws on new polling and analysis of public attitudes and voting behaviour, including among a large sample of ethnic minority voters, to highlight challenges for all political parties and other advocates on this key issue for voters.

The race for representation: how ethnic diversity became the 'new normal' in British politics, *March 2015* analyses the chances of victory of the ethnic minority candidates standing in the 2015 election and makes a series of projections based on different electoral scenarios.

The year of uncertainty: State of the Nation 2015, *January 2015,* looks at the key issues affecting Britain, including the general election and the rise of UKIP; immigration and Europe.

International Students and the UK Immigration Debate, *October 2014*
This joint report with Universities UK examines public attitudes to international students, the largest flow of non-EU migration to the UK. It finds that the public welcomes students and is 'baffled' that they are counted as migrants at all.

Voice of a Generation, *May 2014*
Exploring the most pressing concerns among 17–21 year-olds in the run-up to the 2015 general election, including on party politics, jobs, housing, debt and education.

EU migration from Romania and Bulgaria: What does the public think? *December 2013*

Based on ICM polling and workshops in Southampton, Reading and Bolton, this report examines how much people know about EU migration, their feelings towards EU migrants already here, and what they think could be done in response

From Minority Vote to Majority Challenge, *September 2013*

An analysis of the growing importance of the ethnic minority vote in the UK, including projections as to how the 2010 election could have unfolded if the Conservative Party had secured more votes from ethnic minorities.

Do Mention the War: Will 1914 matter in 2014, *August 2013*

Released one year ahead of the First World War centenary, this report shows that many of us are unsure of what actually happened before, during and after the First World War. Yet most think it is important to seize the opportunity to learn how the First World War shaped the country we are today.

Integration Consensus 1993–2013: How Britain changed since Stephen Lawrence, *April 2013*

This report assesses how much people think the country has changed in the 20 years since Stephen Lawrence's death, showing that while racism appears to have decreased across the country, discrimination still exists.